1989

Happy Birthday Ron
Love
Dad + Mom

Happy Birthday Ron

We Montanans

MICHAEL CRUMMETT

IN CELEBRATION OF
MONTANA'S CENTENNIAL

By Norma Tirrell
Photography by Michael Crummett and others
Foreword by A.B. Guthrie, Jr.

American Geographic Publishing
Helena, Montana

For Robert Tirrell,
who loved the places of Montana,
and for Lillian,
who loves the people.

MICHAEL CRUMMETT

Above: *Veterinarian Greg Tooke on duty.*
Title page: *Centennial paint job on a schoolhouse southeast of Lindsay.*
Cover: *Portraits by Michael Crummett, St. Mary's Lake by Pat O'Hara*

ISBN 0-938314-59-9 (hardbound)
ISBN 0-938314-51-3 (softbound)

© 1988 American Geographic
Publishing
P.O. Box 5630
Helena, Montana 59604
(406) 443-2842

William A. Cordingley, Chairman
Rick Graetz, Publisher
Mark Thompson, Director of Publications
Carolyn Cunningham, Editor,
Montana Magazine
Barbara Fifer, Production Manager

Text © 1988 Norma Tirrell.

Design by Linda McCray.
Printed in Korea by Dong-A Printing Co.

CONTENTS

ACKNOWLEDGMENTS

Author's Acknowledgments

We Montanans is a meld of many people, only some of whom appear on these pages. They are the people who thought that a girl who has spent most of her life in Billings and Helena ought to learn a few more things about Montana before she tries to write a book about it. She ought to witness a calf delivered by caesarean section, for example, or see the Bobcat-Grizzly game from the inside of a locker room or explore Carter County beyond the few miles of blacktop contained within its borders. They are the people who spent hours on the phone or in person, explaining the politics of The Big Open or the economics of Phillips County or the sociology of the North Fork Country.

Among this informal network of advisors, I am especially grateful to my agriculture round table: Doc Curtis, T.J. Gilles, Nancy Matheson and Greg Tooke for educating me on the likes of botanicals, brome and buffalo grass; and Jennifer Tully and Rock Ringling for evaluating my perceptions of the rural lifestyle.

Over the past year, I relied on regional advisors who opened doors, sent files and newspaper clips, gave guided tours and generally went out of their way to show me around their communities. Among them are: Sally Thompson, Janice Downey, Marilyn Maney, Marko Lucich, April Milroy, Polly Wischmann, Marilyn Wessel, Jim Peterson, Becky Tirrell, Alice Finnegan, Bea McCarthy, Jan Dunbar and Dr. Henry McClernan.

Jim Posewitz counseled me on a range of issues, from football to the history of the conservation movement. Governor Ted Schwinden knows Indians as neighbors and negotiators; I am grateful for his insights. I leaned heavily on University of Montana professors Tony Beltramo and Gertrude Lackschewitz for their considerable research on Montana's ethnic and immigration patterns; historian Richard Roeder for his knowledge of the development of literature and the arts, and oral historian Laurie Mercier for contacts throughout the state. I am grateful to Janine Pease Windy Boy for teaching me a great deal about my own culture by telling me about hers.

I have new appreciation for librarians, especially Jan Clack, formerly of the Montana Census & Economic Information Center; Bruce Newell, the "information cowboy" at Lewis & Clark Library, and Dave Walter, who seems to carry the entire contents of the Montana Historical Society Library inside his head.

My thanks to Mark Thompson for knowing all along where this book was going but allowing me to figure it out for myself, to Rick Graetz for giving me the opportunity to rediscover my native state and to Barbara Fifer for keeping track of too many drafts. To Mike Crummett for his ability to capture a sense of place in his images of people. To Paula Walker for demonstrating that a good editor can remain a good friend. To John Wilson for accommodating this project; Susan Hansen for listening to it, and Gordon Bennett for living with it and encouraging it every day.

Finally, my thanks to the Montanans who welcomed me into their homes and onto their farms and ranches; who set an extra plate for me and walked me through their photo albums; whose love of Montana rekindled my own.

—*Norma Tirrell*

JOHN REDDY

The geometry of strip farming in North-central Montana.

Photographer's Acknowledgments

I owe my heartfelt thanks to many!

To Mark Thompson and Norma Tirrell, who challenged me to fulfill an enduring dream—to photograph the spirit, strength and diversity of Montana's people.

I'm obliged to the countless Montanans who, for the last 12 years, have permitted me to poke my third eye into your lives and schedules. Without you, there would be no celebration, Centennial or otherwise.

Mostly, I am indebted to my family—Linda, Justin, Nathan, Shep and Greyson—for allowing me to get so involved in these lengthy, all-consuming, away-from-home undertakings.

—Michael Crummett

TOM DIETRICH

Hutterite farm near Conrad.

Quotations & Other Borrowed Material

Montana: High, Wide, and Handsome, by Joseph Kinsey Howard, Preface by A.B. Guthrie, Jr., © 1943, 1959 by Yale University Press.

"You tramp across the ridgeline...," song and lyrics by Walkin' Jim Stoltz, reprinted by permission of the author.

"The Missouri" and "Ode to the Other," poems by Greg Keeler, reprinted by permission of the author from *American Falls*, Confluence Press, 1987.

Today I Baled Some Hay to Feed the Sheep the Coyotes Eat, by Bill Stockton, Falcon Press, 1983. Drawings reprinted by permission of the artist.

"Farm & Ranch Trib," *Great Falls Tribune*, various columns by T.J. Gilles. Statements reprinted by permission of the publisher.

Travels With Charley, by John Steinbeck, © 1962 by John Steinbeck. Reprinted by permission of Viking Penguin, Inc.

"David Shaner: Montana Conversation," *The Studio Potter* (Goffstown, N.H.), Vol. 8, No. 1, 1979.

"David Shaner," by Daniel Rhodes, *American Craft* (New York, N.Y.), Feb.-March, 1983.

"Letter from Montana: A Cheap Hide-Out for Writers," by David Quammen, *The New York Times Book Review*, Nov. 1, 1981.

The Death of Jim Loney, by James Welch, Penguin Books, New York, N.Y., 1987.

"Pamelia: From Pioneer to Prima Donna," by Linda Peavy and Ursula Smith, *Montana Artpaper*, Fall 1987.

"Reincarnation," poem by Wallace McRae, reprinted by permission of the author from *It's Just Grass and Water*, © 1976, 1980, 1986 by Shaun Higgins, Oxalis Group, Spokane, Washington.

PREFACE

When Montana is in one of its economic funks, it is somehow easier to think the unthinkable: Life on the outside. After all these years, should I go?

The grass was looking considerably greener elsewhere a year ago when talk of Montana's statehood centennial began to dominate the conversations and "to do" lists of merchants, art dealers and book publishers. The folks at Montana Magazine/American Geographic Publishing had an interesting angle. Why not produce a book about the people of Montana? Not a history or a geograhry but a contemporary view of a people. A mirror, in effect, to hold up to the people of Montana on the occasion of their state's 100th birthday.

Reason enough to put my vagrant thoughts on hold. The world could wait one more year.

My year is up, and here I am, rooted like sagebrush to my Montana home. It has been a year of discovery for a native who thought she knew her state. A year of diversity for a white, European descendant who thought we Montanans were all alike. A year of awakening for an urbanite who thought agriculture was a yawn. And a year of romance for a realist who thought all that cowboy stuff was hype.

A year later, I find myself combing the farm and ranch calendar that appears in the Sunday Great Falls Tribune, and making plans to attend the four-county Marias Fair in Shelby and the sheep and wool festival in Bozeman. I'm reading up on wild turkey lore in anticipation of a trip to the Bull Mountains that couldn't be squeezed in this year. I can't miss the wedding of a new friend at the Turner Hutterite Colony. Or the Montana premiere of "Pamelia," an opera written and composed by three Montanans.

A year later, I catch myself analyzing names and listening for accents that betray foreign ancestry. Croatian Mesopust, the annual Dutch Dinner at Churchill and Missoula's Greek Festival have gained a permanent spot on my personal calendar of events.

Best of all, I enjoy easy rapport across the state simply by knowing the vet in Malta or the grocer in Sand Springs. In Montana, a little influence goes a long way. Among the highlights of the past year were the infrequent sessions with photographer Mike Crummett, reviewing sleeves and carousels of color transparencies—lovely images of the people I had interviewed. It was like seeing old friends again. Montana Folklorist Michael Korn has described Montana as "one big neighborhood that just happens to have a lot of country between houses."

The Montana neighborhood is peopled with a surprising diversity of characters whose common bond is their unspeakable attachment to their state. If there is something truly different about Montana—something that won't let go—it is the people who won't let go of Montana.

—*Norma Tirrell*
June 1988

MICHAEL CRUMMETT PHOTO

FOREWORD

The aim of this noteworthy book by Norma Tirrell is to explain Montana and Montanans, not just to Montanans themselves but to readers at large. In the making of it the author traveled to all sections of the state and talked to all manner of people, gathering the flavor of places and the outlooks of men and women of different racial and ethnic origins and different experiences.

The result is an illuminating, many-faceted study that readers will find steadily interesting.

It is not my intention to deal more with this work. It speaks for itself. What I have to say constitutes a brief addition, written from a different approach. It is one man's conclusions from the history of the state, and it is history I must begin with.

For me the story of the territory and state begins with the coming of the fur trader and trapper, who were drawn here because beaver were plenty. I dismiss for my purposes the expedition of Lewis and Clark and their men, who stayed long enough, going to the Pacific and coming from there, to name many streams, numerous rock formations and some sections of landscape. But they were, after all, birds of passage, their importance here lying only in the excitement they caused among the fur people of St. Louis, the starting point for trading parties and source of venture capital for western enterprises.

But the fur hunter, the mountain man of legend, came and stayed long enough that something of his spirit still lives. Witness the few who still trap the streams or, varying the field, snare coyotes. Witness the many who gather at "rendezvous," men dressed in buckskins, carrying their muzzle loaders with which to match skills.

Only six short years after Lewis and Clark returned to St. Louis, the first trading post in Montana sat on the banks of the lower Yellowstone. Called Fort Lisa, or Manuel, it was an enterprise of Manuel Lisa, a St. Louis Spaniard with an interest in the trade and the money to invest. Included in the venture were a number of his paid trappers. They stand in contrast to the "free" trappers who gambled on their catches and the prices to be paid.

Lisa's undertaking was the forerunner of others on the upper Missouri into Montana. More trading posts followed his, both on the big river and on the Yellowstone. Up from St. Louis sailed the keelboats, daring the mad Missouri, carriers of traders and trappers and their supplies. "Sailed" is hardly the word. Rather, the boats were worked upstream by poles, ropes and oars, seldom by sail for the winds weren't constant. It was brutal toil, but the French boatmen stayed merry. They sang songs as they labored. They were half beaver themselves, so the word was. There was need of good nature, fighting this crazy flow. It made changes in its channel. It altered itself, bank to bank. It brought dead trees and floating islands of sand with willows rising thick from them. A sunken log could erupt as a boat passed over, puncturing the craft, spilling contents and crew. Season to season the river changed, piling up sand bars where the channel was clear one year before. A restless water, that sure enough was the Missouri.

And the travelers had to watch out for Indians. They shied away from

NORMA TIRRELL

A modern "mountain man."

high banks where arrows might rain down on them. When they could, they tied up for the night at islands, where the danger of trouble was lessened.

Hardships and dangers regardless, the travelers arrived. Fort Union, near the junction of the Yellowstone and Missouri, almost on the border between Montana and South Dakota, came into being. Financed and manned by the American Fur Company, it became one of the famous posts of the west.

It fathered Fort Piegan, upstream in real Blackfoot country. That post was short-lived, located on the wrong bank of the river. Still farther up, Fort Union begat Fort McKenzie. Bad management and fire put an end to it. Then, after an abortive try too far up the stream, Fort Benton came into being. It was the final post built on the Missouri, final because boats encountered too many difficulties beyond it. Indeed, about 40 miles farther on was the Great Falls of the Missouri.

As head of navigation Fort Benton prospered, becoming in time more important than Fort Union. Even steamboats, successors to keelboats, got there, except for a few that had to tie up at Cow Island, from where their cargoes were freighted by team to Fort Benton. The river steamboats, some wag commented, were of such shallow draft that they could sail on dew.

Some of those fur hunters who had come overland along the Platte valley ventured north in the spring after wintering in Colorado or Utah. They crossed over the "bad pass" above the Little Bighorn and came to the Yellowstone. They trapped that river and its tributary where the Crow Indians, although thievish, gave little trouble. But the Blackfeet in the neighborhood of the Three Forks of the Missouri were savage. They did to death any party or parties who ventured into that territory. The fur hunters soon learned to fight shy of it.

The real heyday of the mountain man was short, from about 1820 to about 1840. He had been too good a trapper, so good that the remaining beaver were few, hardly worth the effort of catching. More than that, market prices for pelts fell almost to nothing. Those swells in London had come to prefer silk hats to beaver. Some mountain men hung on for a time, but their numbers kept dwindling, reaching virtual zero at last.

It is easy but not accurate to say they left nothing of consequence behind them. They discovered routes and natural wonders that later men were to follow and marvel at. They passed on some knowledge of how to get along with the Indians; and the French, the most adaptable of all, left descendants from their unions with Indian women. Today Montanans with French names are so common as to be unremarkable. The mountain man left a legend and a great hunger among many American males for the old, free life in unspoiled country.

When, years later, the Missouri river trade in Montana had come to nothing and the American Fur Company had departed, many of its employees stayed on in Montana, going to the towns, small and big, that were sprouting. The clerks, men of more than common education, became respected citizens. Often they filled county offices.

But business at the trading posts didn't depend on beaver alone. As the harvest of fine furs diminished, business grew and developed with buffalo hides, the despised coarse fur of the mountain man. The company shipped

MICHAEL CRUMMETT

At a celebration on Rocky Boy's Reservation.

thousands and thousands of hides, along with uncounted buffalo tongues, both of which commanded a ready market in the east. The buffalo tongues were the only meat the hunters saved. The rest lay waste on the plains, free meals for coyotes and wolves. Later, human scavengers were to gather the bones for fertilizer plants.

So Fort Benton and Fort Union thrived, and Fort Benton thrived all the more as the point of supply for miners with the discoveries of gold in the early 1860s. There it was, in the gravel of Grasshopper Creek, found in 1862, and Bannack City sprang up. Then in Alder Gulch, discovered the next year, then in Last Chance Gulch and Confederate Gulch. Thousands streamed to the diggings, gold pans and shovels in hand. Virginia City was founded and Helena, as well as settlements like Bannack, ghost towns of today.

Miners had to eat, and the range cattle business came from that necessity. The plains grass was free, thanks to the federal government that owned it, and cattle, unfed, could survive the winters without crippling losses to ranchers. Nothing to it. Stock the ranges. But the winter of 1886-1887 came along, and perhaps half the cattle in Montana died of cold and starvation. The losses were total in some cases. Granville Stuart, partner in one big enterprise, quit the business, unable to endure such creature suffering. The industry survived once men were reconciled to fences and the need to feed hay. The hired hand led a mean and dirty life, but there he was, on horseback, and so the legend of the cowboy caught people's imagination, as it does today.

Along with cattle ranching, sheep growing became big business. Sheep, the golden hoof, as bankers and investors came to call them. The business didn't shrink until sometime in the 1940s. Bands of a thousand or more animals demanded herders, sheep being unable to watch out for themselves, and herders and the necessary summer pasturage became hard to find. Today for the most part sheep are kept under fence in small numbers. The herder left no grand illusions. He was a solitary man, probably by choice, and, more important, he was afoot. He left sheepherders' monuments, rock cairns built on hills, once a common sight in Montana. For the rest, he left a reputation for thirst and an acknowledged devotion to his charges. More than one herder died in storms while trying to save his sheep.

In time the gold fields gave up their treasure and the buffalo were largely gone, reduced from their one-time thousands to a solitary few by 1883. And the railroads had come, the Utah and Northern, a branch line of the Union Pacific in 1869, the Northern Pacific in 1881 and the Great Northern in 1887. But even before they penetrated Montana, Fort Union and Fort Benton were done as ports. It was cheaper to freight goods from railheads to the east than to bring them up the tortuous miles of the Missouri. Fort Benton became the small, pleasant little place it is today and Fort Union a park.

Almost coincident with the advent of railroads there came Indian "battles," so-called though only one of them qualified. In January of 1870 Major Eugene Baker led a detachment of cavalry from Fort Shaw to the broken banks of the Marias where the troops slaughtered men, women and children of an unoffending band sickened by smallpox. They appropriated the horse herd, burned the tepees and left a few surviving women and children to make out if they could on the freezing plains.

MICHAEL CRUMMETT

A newly-shorn flock.

Montana cheered the massacre. By God, the troops had made good Injuns of the Blackfeet by making them dead.

The one actual battle was the Battle of the Little Bighorn in June of 1876 where the Sioux and Cheyennes triumphed over General Custer by killing him and all the troops he had saved for the general attack. The Indians won, but the fight marked the end of their old, free tribal life on the plains. The enemy was too many, the white men as uncountable as the blades of grass.

Chief Joseph and his Nez Perces made their historic retreat out of Idaho into Montana the following year, making fools of their military pursuers and white defenders alike. General Nelson A. Miles caught them and subdued them in the Bear Paws, 40 miles from the Canadian border.

The year 1885 marked the end of the Riel rebellion in Canada. Riel's followers and sympathizers drifted south into Montana. Chippewas, Crees and Métis, they came to be called landless Indians because they had no reservations. They had a sorry time of it, extending well into this century.

BRUCE SELYEM

From gold the miners turned to silver and from silver to copper. That was the thing, copper. And there in an elbow of the divide rose the richest hill on earth. Almost on its shoulder Butte was built. Butte, the boisterous city, in Montana but hardly of it, a place in itself where people of many nations gathered and wrangled. Butte, home of the copper kings, who plundered the hill and sought to plunder one another, until Standard Oil took over the properties and became the political czar of Montana.

The bequest of Standard Oil is, I hope, an abiding resistance to corporate control of the state. We learned from Marcus Daly, William A. Clark, Frederick Augustus Heinze and the Anaconda Copper Company, alias Standard Oil. It was both a sad and a happy day in Montana when the copper was gone, the company fading in importance and its controlled newspapers sold.

Homesteaders had been coming to Montana, and with the railroads to use they came in flocks. Untried would-be farmers and bookkeepers from the east, Swedes and Norwegians from Minnesota and the old country, Germans, Scotsmen, Englishmen, Russians, immigrants from a dozen countries—all answering to the hope of a better life. Rain followed the plow, so it was said, and Jim Hill of the Great Northern had advertisements showing greenbacks in the turned soil.

Hope begat towns, would-be cities, certain-to-be cities. They came to life where the railroads ran. Promoters platted town lots that came to lie dusty in their old files. There were the beginnings of wheat elevators. Along the Great Northern's high line from Havre to Shelby lie little towns and the remainders of towns, many with English names, for Jim Hill liked to please English investors. Spurs extended from the main lines, and here, too, dreams got their names. In my own section I can name half a dozen off hand—Manchester, Ashuelot, Gilman, Claude, Coyle, Agawam.

It was a time of high hope, the first decade of this century. Men felt buoyant. A good life was certain. Don't hold the horses. I can remember the Teton County Silver Cornet Band, in which my dad played the tuba, belting out, "You bet your boots, you beat the band, Montana Land, Montana Land." The tune was "Maryland, My Maryland," itself a borrowing from a much older song.

*   *   *

I have traced Montana's history because we are all part of what has gone before. In us is some of the spirit of the mountain man, some of the expectation of the prospector, some of the cowboy's liking for boots, choke-bore pants, a big hat and a horse. Some of the endurance of the homesteader, a bit of this and a bit of that, and perhaps deep and dormant in those of us without trace of Indian blood, a guilty sorrow at the treatment of the red man. All of what we are we owe to our forerunners. The same distances please our eyes, the same heights lift our spirits, the same streams invite our rods and the same fields our guns. The same sun puts squints in our eyes, and the same winds scour our faces, and we answer to sight and sound and prospect as they did. Our history lives in us.

Outsiders may ask: Why live in Montana, where winters are rough, wind almost a constant, and livelihood dependent on a fickle climate?

We stutter over an answer, never having quite formulated one. We know we like space, like room for the eye and the mind. On the plains a butte floats against the distant horizon. In the west the mountains lift. The streams are there with fish in them, and in the open fields and in the hills game lives, and an elk bugles. If we travel to the west or east coasts we are appalled and repelled by the traffic and the crowds. The air stinks and the water tastes funny. Give us Montana. That's home.

What then besides? What is a Montanan? How does he differ? I would put friendliness first. Here is no cold indifference, no short and harsh answer, if any, to the visitor's question. The tourist is welcomed, first because he is human, not because he has money to spend. That's important but secondary. In a pinch the sheriff will open a gas station to help, and the man in the pickup will stop to ask if the stranded traveler is all right. I believe this characteristic comes from the sparsity of population. Crowds make for discourtesy.

To further define a Montanan:

He is a writer in Missoula and a sheepherder in the Big Dry. He is an executive with the Montana Power Company in Butte and a line repairman in Billings. He is a school teacher in Havre and a trout-fly maker in Livingston. All right, if you prefer, she is a ranch wife in Chouteau County and a state legislator in Bozeman. She is a computer operator in Great Falls, a Forest Service spokesman in Helena and a cowgirl in Pony.

Yep, we're all of these things.

Add that we are a hopeful people, we Montanans. If things go bad, surely they'll be better next year. Hang on and see. Yes, sir, you wait and see. So we endure, and hope is alive in us. If anyone wants to find us, here we are.

                                                —*A.B. Guthrie, Jr.*

Tipi reflection on the Flathead Reservation.

MICHAEL CRUMMETT

Near Helmville.

1

WHO ARE
WE MONTANANS?

At first glance, we Montanans seem to be alike. With few exceptions, we look alike, talk alike, celebrate the same holidays and honor the same traditions.

But you don't have to dig deep or drive far to expose our rich diversity. Throughout the state, pockets of Germans, Greeks and Finns still speak their mother tongues with some regularity. Well over 90 percent of Montana's Crow Indians speak their native language; for them, English is a second language. But on the Flathead Reservation in Western Montana, teachers and cultural leaders are working hard to revive their native language before it vanishes.

On Billings' south side, the Hispanic community celebrates El Cinco de Mayo—the May 5th anniversary of the defeat of an invading French army by Mexican peasants in 1862—with Mexican foods, costume and dance. Butte Serbians gather at their Eastern Orthodox Church on January 6, their

Missoula businessman Dan Lambros auctions gifts at Missoula's annual Greek Festival.

Christmas Eve, for the ceremonial burning of the Yule Log, or "Badnjak." In neighboring Anaconda, a sizeable Croatian community prepares for the Lenten season by burning in effigy a life-size dummy that personifies all the evil that has occurred during the past year. Miles City's many Scots celebrate their heritage every January at the Bobby Burns Dance, complete with Caledonian pipe bands and dancers. And everyone who makes it to Butte on March 17 is an Irishman, if only for a day.

Far from homogeneous, Montanans are a meld of many nations, primarily European and white. Germans make up the single, largest ethnic group, followed by people who trace their ancestry to the British Isles and the Scandinavian countries. Smaller groups, still distinct, are French, Dutch, Italians, Greeks, Slavs, Asians and people of Spanish origin. All were preceded by Montana's earliest settlers, the Indians, who now comprise roughly five percent of the state's population.

More visible than Montanans' ethnic differences are our geographic differences. It is difficult to say where Eastern Montana ends and Central and Western Montana begin, but somewhere east of Lewistown, along about the lower Musselshell River and the UL Bend country, the sociology of Montana changes dramatically. Pickups become "outfits," and a young man's fancy turns from Ford Mustangs to buckin' horses. Circles of acquaintances grow wider, and news travels faster than home delivery of the

Right: *Playing grown-up at the Turner Hutterite Colony.*
Below: *Crow Fair Parade.*
Bottom: *Jose Arredondo pauses at the Hispanic mural that adorns Billings' Koinonia Restaurant & Gathering Place.*

MICHAEL CRUMMETT PHOTOS BOTH PAGES

4

Billings Gazette when a wrangler from Malta meets a rancher from Miles City at a Hereford sale in Billings.

The schemes and dreams that lured Montana's first settlers are as varied as the people who pursued them. Whether it was beaver pelts, gold nuggets, rich grass or free acreage, the schemes were generally of the get-rich-quick variety, and a few of the dreamers did just that. The vast majority merely got wise quickly to the fact that Montana was a fickle land. Their fortunes came no more easily here than anywhere else they had been; in some cases, they came harder. Many disappeared as quickly as they had arrived. But those who stayed and stuck it out set the standard for those Montanans who followed. If we Montanans are anything, we are survivors.

Cascade County home extension agent Claire Del Guerra is amused by the nation's insatiable appetite for pasta and wonders why it took Americans so long to discover the simple elegance of the food she grew up with. "We've been doing this for years, haven't we?" she said to her mother, Olanda Vangelisti of Black Eagle. Olanda, known as "Nonna" or Grandma to her friends and family, is famous for the homemade soups, sauces and "ravs" she has been turning out for nearly 40 years at Eddie's Supper Club in Great Falls.

Claire remembers pasta, fresh vegetables and homemade wine as staples of the Vangelisti kitchen. "Carloads of grapes" came into Black Eagle and people could choose from "bins of different varieties" of pasta at half a dozen Italian markets, Olanda recalled of the once-thriving smelter town of Black Eagle.

"It is different now," she said of the town once known as "Little Chicago" because of its ethnic, blue-collar mix. "We were all like one family."

Besides smelter workers, the Black Eagle family included the families of smelter officials who lived on the hill overlooking the community. There was never any doubt about who was superior, according to Claire, but somehow the classes lived together in harmony. "They were the officials, and we had tremendous respect for them," she said. "But they felt the same way about us. They loved our food and wine."

Before he died in 1949, Claire's father, Dante Vangelisti, worked as gardener and groundskeeper at the Anaconda smelter. In addition to his responsibility for the smelter grounds, where he planted colorful bulb gardens in the shape of the company's copper arrowhead, Dante maintained the tennis courts and ice skating ponds for the families of smelter officials. Every year he put up the company Christmas tree and nativity scene.

"He used to take bouquets of fresh flowers to the wives of the smelter officials every day," Olanda recalled. Claire, who inherited an Italian love of gardens and growing things, remembers her father as a gifted gardener and loyal employee: "He wanted everything to reflect the beauty of the plant, the company, because he was so proud to be an employee of the Anaconda Company."

MICHAEL CRUMMETT

Olanda Vangelisti, left, and her daughter, Claire Del Guerra, remember when there were half a dozen Italian markets in the once-thriving smelter town of Black Eagle.

Bob Milodragovich, *retired forester, Missoula, formerly of Butte:*
"A mining town doesn't grow; it erupts."

JOHN REDDY PHOTOS

Above: *St. Patrick's Day is as close as Butte Irish get to heaven on earth.*
Left: *One of Butte's most notable Finns is Ervin Niemi, owner of the Helsinki Bar & Steam Bath.*

She described the smelter's 506-foot-tall stack, which was removed from the Great Falls skyline in 1982 when Anaconda closed out its Montana operations, as "the core of our community, a beautiful part of our lives."

Living in a barracks, sharing a bathhouse with several families and fighting dust storms hardly constitute an enviable lifestyle, but for Eugene and Lucile Best, the hardships they endured in 1935, during their first year of the Fort Peck Dam construction project, are among the happiest memories of their lives. Now retired in Glasgow, they are confident that "everyone else who worked on the project would say the same."

It was a good time to be alive. The United States was working again. Thousands of Depression-era workers found employment on the huge public works project. Paychecks were coming regularly and booze was flowing again. Prohibition was over.

The work was dangerous and it was hard. "If a guy didn't work like hell, they canned you," said Eugene, who started in 1935 as a surveyor and retired in 1969 as an administrative officer for the entire project.

"Laborers hired out for 50 cents a day, and they provided their own pick and shovel," he said. "And they were happy to get that," Lucile added. "You made friends easily because everyone was in the same boat. Everyone was equal, and it was an ideal place to raise a family for that reason."

Glasgow residents Eugene and Lucile Best are happy to have been a part of the Fort Peck Dam construction project.

But Lucile was apprehensive when they first arrived on the project. She and Eugene had been living in Gardiner, where he worked seasonally as a surveyor in Yellowstone Park. "We needed full-time work but when we got to Fort Peck, I thought it was the end of the world," she said, recalling her initial exposure to drought, dust storms and grasshoppers. "Every morning, I swept dust and sand off my kitchen table," she said, "but after a couple of visits to Gardiner, I realized I was anxious to get back home."

Gardiner was a good training ground for Fort Peck, according to Lucile, because it was "pretty wild" in those days, too, but in Fort Peck, "I saw things I never thought I would see. Every class of people came, and everyone was just so happy to have money."

The Fort Peck Dam project made life larger for those who were there, and Eugene and Lucile know it. They mean it when they say, "We wouldn't trade it for anything."

Bill Caras belongs to a small but visible community of Greek families in Missoula. It would be easy to dismiss Montana's Greeks, whose numbers are small, except that their stature is large. It is not enough that they are successful, well established merchants and professionals; many have risen to leadership positions within their professions.

The owner of Caras Nursery and Landscape, Bill Caras is a former president of the Montana Association of Nurserymen and is on his way to

Above: A model Indian enterprise, A & S Industries employs 450 workers on the Fort Peck Indian Reservation.
Top: These field workers are semi-permanent members of Billings' Hispanic community.
Left: Kids find common ground at Crow Fair.

8

becoming president of the National Landscape Association. His father and uncle are both past presidents of the Montana Florist Association. Bill attributes the Greek will to succeed more to the first generation of Greek immigrants than to their descendants. He prefers to recount the aspirations and accomplishments of his late grandfather James Caras than to dwell on his own.

Like many Greeks, Jim Caras dreamed of owning his own business when he arrived in America shortly after the turn of the century. He decided early on that he would open a flower shop so that he could deal with a "high class of people." When he first arrived in Missoula, he joined about 100 other Greeks who worked for the Northern Pacific Railroad. He later owned a coffee house, a candy shop and a fresh produce store before getting into the flower business in 1911. In a biography, Bill's grandfather revealed ingenious means of staying one step ahead of bill collectors and confessed that he used to dab violet perfume from Woolworth's on his road-weary California violets to make them more appealing to his customers. In 1921, he bought the facilities and land that later became one of the leading greenhouses in the Pacific Northwest. The Caras floral empire has since grown into three Missoula businesses, Caras Nursery and Landscape, Garden City Floral and Webber Wholesale Florists.

Bill and Laurie Caras are active members of Missoula's Greek community.

According to Bill, his grandfather's greatest achievement was his ability to provide a good education for his children and subsequent generations of Carases.

A new life out West was no life for Verna Carlson's mother, but Verna flowered under the Eastern Montana sun. She weathered its winters as well, and now, looking back from the vantage point of her 90-plus years, Verna is at peace with the notion that "you learn to get out of life what you can when you can."

The homesteader's life on the isolated plains north of Circle drove Verna's mother away but Verna chose to stay. "We were fools," she said of her family's trip from Indiana to Montana in 1910 to stake their claim under the Enlarged Homestead Act of 1909. "The railroads bragged up their land out here, and my dad swallowed all of that," she said. "When we arrived on the first of November, there was nothing on our homestead but native grass. We camped in a nine-by-ten tent, then lived in an unfinished house until Dad finished our dugout."

In 1913, Verna married a cowboy working on the nearby Conrad Kohrs ranch, and they homesteaded at Prairie Elk, picking up enough "stray stuff"—patches of land and rough country—to put together a small grain and livestock operation.

Homesteader Verna Carlson remembers the good times at Prairie Elk, north of Circle.

Verna has vivid recall of the hard times—the isolation, the dust, the magpies, the drudgery of hauling water, the Depression. But what she dwells

We Montanans

Above: *Greek festival, the view from the kitchen.*
Left: *Guests enjoy authentic Greek cuisine.*
Below: *Missoula's Greeks love a good party.*

on are the good times. There were the Fourth of·July celebrations at Sand Creek that lasted two days, the country dances where she played the piano, "sometimes until my fingers bled," and the Farmers Union, which enlarged Verna's world well beyond Prairie Elk and her eighth-grade education.

Verna was active in the Farmers Union from the 1920s to the 1950s. For 14 years, she served as the organization's director of education for McCone County. "I ran around quite a lot in those days," she recalled with a smile. "We had speakers and lectures, winter schools for leaders and summer camps for kids. We practiced our public speaking so we didn't feel so backwoodsy when we went to town."

Thinking back to the plains of Prairie Elk from the comfort of her home in Circle, Verna views her move to town with inherent good cheer: "I liked country life. I didn't think I would ever live in town. But a little town can be precious to you, too. I've got friends forever."

Paul Ringling, rancher, Carter County:

"People in Eastern Montana at least know where Missoula and Kalispell are."

In his own words, Jose Chavez has made it. He has "a nice house in Billings Heights, two cars and a great job." So why does he spend nights and weekends on Billings' south side, coaching underdog kids in a boxing ring? It is not just because they need something to do, someone to look up to. He needs them, too.

"Before I got started working with these kids, I was a couch potato," said the energetic safety supervisor of the Conoco Refinery as he tried to sit still long enough to explain his mission. "I had a drinking problem, I was depressed and I was critical of everything. Today, I feel 100 percent better. Instead of cursing the darkness, I decided to light a candle."

Chavez decided he wanted to help kids after working as a correctional officer in the New Mexico State Penitentiary. "Most of the prison population was Hispanic or some minority," he said. "I felt sorry for their kids because they didn't have any say over where they were born. It wasn't their fault they would wind up as criminals. That's all they knew."

Chavez found the same pattern when he moved to Billings more than 20 years ago. Many of the Hispanic kids on the south side were being raised by aunts and grandparents. "They visit their dads in Deer Lodge," he said.

Jose Chavez puts in another evening with members of the Billings Amateur Boxing Association.

It was the lack of male role models that inspired Chavez to form the Billings Amateur Boxing Association. "All these kids know is fighting, stealing and lying," he said. "Boxing is one way to teach them how to use their energy in a positive way."

Chavez spends two hours a night in the ring; on weekends, he takes the club to out-of-town meets. The kids understand that if they drop out of school or let their grades slip, they are out of the ring.

Like others involved in corrections, Chavez puts in many hours for few rewards. But the rewards are there. "When I see a kid getting better grades or going to church or walking a little differently, I know he's feeling better about himself," he said. "Some of these kids go to bed with their boxing trophies."

Their ancestors were nomadic hunters, drawn to the Great Plains by its life-sustaining buffalo herds, but today Assiniboine and Sioux Indians make

Right: *Music makes the job more bearable for Adriana Vela.*
Below: *Boxing starts at an early age on Billings' south side.*
Bottom: *Hispanic Little League teams play at Billings' South Park.*

MICHAEL CRUMMETT PHOTOS BOTH PAGES

ends meet as oil producers and defense contractors. Putting in a shift at A & S Industries, which produces camouflage material and metal storage boxes for the Defense Department, is a drastic departure from the tribes' ancestral occupation but, according to Fort Peck tribal leader Norman Hollow, it accomplishes the same end. The self-esteem that comes from making a living has restored pride to the residents of the Fort Peck Indian Reservation.

A & S is a model Indian enterprise, and if any single person made it possible, it is Hollow, who has served more than 40 years on the Fort Peck Tribal Council, 12 of them as tribal chairman. A skillful politician, Hollow went after the camouflage contract in 1973, cultivating the influence of U.S. Senate Majority Leader Mike Mansfield and a North Dakota senator to turn the minority-bound contract away from the more powerful black lobby to two obscure Indian reservations in Montana and North Dakota.

Above: *Former Fort Peck Tribal Chairman Norman Hollow is one of Montana's most highly respected Indian leaders.*
Facing page: *As the Berkeley Pit grew, it replaced Butte's underground mines and the immigrant hardrock miners who found work in them.*

Jim Curtis, D.V.M., Malta:
"To understand an Eastern Montanan, you just need to know the most commonly asked question in Eastern Montana, and that's, 'How much moisture did we get last month?'"

"They were hesitant to award the contract to us because of all that they had heard about lazy Indians and high absenteeism rates," Hollow said 15 years later. "But I convinced them to give us a chance, and we haven't missed a production deadline yet."

A & S employs about 450 workers on the reservation, including about 20 percent non-Indians, and figures heavily in the tribes' standing as having one of the lowest Indian unemployment rates in the region.

Hollow also gets the credit for successfully negotiating the nation's first water rights compact between a state and an Indian reservation, but you won't hear about it from him. He is a quiet leader. "When I first got involved in tribal affairs, I was pretty vocal," he said. "My dad gave me some advice: 'Don't speak and talk about your accomplishments; people have the eyes to see them and the ears to hear them. Go about it quietly'."

If Hollow won't articulate his accomplishments, Vera, his wife of 50 years, will. She will volunteer that Hollow was inducted into the Indian Hall of Fame in 1981, that attorneys call him regularly for his opinions and interpretations of treaty rights and that he is the only Indian on the reservation who still knows how to tie a star knot. A Danish woman from Froid, Vera met Norman in high school at Culbertson. "My mother was very opposed to the marriage at first," she recalled. "But it didn't take her long to realize that no one could touch him."

Montana's Yugoslavs are easily recognized. They are the "ich's" and they are everywhere. Descended from the people of the war-torn Balkan States in southeastern Europe, they trace their roots to a nation that did not even exist until 1918, after their ancestors had immigrated to America. Hence their allegiance to Croatia, Serbia or the other "nations" that formed Yugoslavia after World War I.

When they first arrived in Montana, the Slavs found work in the mines and smelters of Butte and Anaconda. Many also settled in Red Lodge, Billings, Lewistown and Black Eagle. But they regarded their industrial jobs as transitional and devoted themselves to the pursuit of education and better jobs elsewhere.

MICHAEL CRUMMETT PHOTOS BOTH PAGES

Bob Milodragovich and his brothers found a "better life" with the U.S. Forest Service.

Two products of that ethnic search for a better life are Bob Milodragovich, a retired U.S. Forest Service officer living in Missoula, and Louie Yovetich, a retired railroad engineer and former mayor of Laurel. Both are Butte natives, the sons of miners who wanted something better for their children.

According to Bob, it is not surprising that all the Milodragovich boys wound up working for the Forest Service. "We all wanted to be forest rangers," he said. "Fortunately, we had a high school advisor who knew that foresters did not live by a creek and ride a white horse. She steered us in the right direction by getting us into the sciences—chemistry and physics." By the time he had retired in 1972, Bob had worked as a ranger on three Montana forests, a staff officer on two Wyoming forests, a forest supervisor in Colorado and an administrator in Washington, D.C. It would be hard for him to choose his favorite assignment because he loved them all. "I feel about the Forest Service the way Marines feel about the Marines," he said. "There are no ex-Marines."

In Laurel, Yovetich developed a similar love affair with the railroad. "As a third grader in Butte, I dreamed that some day I'd be able to work on a steam engine," he said. By 17, he was working in the mines, but on his day off, he worked for the railroad. He said he talked his way into a full-time job and stayed there 41 years, 34 as an engineer. During that time, Louie ran freight trains, passenger trains, locals and switch engines. Like Milodragovich, he loved it all, but railroading for Louie was never the same after the steam engine. "Those engines talked to you; they were part of your life," he said. "Climbing into a diesel engine was like getting into a car with an automatic shift."

Still, he was grateful for a good-paying job that enabled him, in the best Slavic tradition, to educate his kids. "I was thankful for the privilege of working for the railroad," he said.

Both "ich's" speak the Serbo-Croatian language and can retell their parents' immigration stories as if they were their own. Their fathers both suffered from silicosis, or "miners' con" (consumption). Louie's dad died of it. Bob's dad got out of the mines before it killed him. Both men served in World War II; Bob put in another year in Korea. "As immigrant descendants in Butte, we had a deep, abiding love of this country," he said. "Our parents taught us that they came here to find a better life."

Former Laurel Mayor Louie Yovetich left Butte to fulfill his dream of working for the railroad.

Retired coal miner John Kastelitz recalls the details of one of Montana's worst underground mine explosions as if it happened yesterday. In fact, it has been nearly 50 years since the Smith Mine Disaster, together with changing markets, technology and transportation, signaled the end of Carbon County's once-booming coal mining industry.

It was February 27, 1943. Miners at the Bearcreek mine were working around the clock to produce coal for the war effort. At 9:30 a.m., a methane gas explosion killed 30 miners instantly. Another 44 bodies were recovered during the days to come. One of the rescue workers was Kastelitz, who had been working the afternoon shift.

A sprawling state depends on rail transportation to move commodities like coal, grain and lumber.

"We waited until night to bring most of the bodies out so there wouldn't be so many spectators," Kastelitz recalled. "Most couldn't be identified; they were identified only by their miner's tag." Among the bodies he helped remove from the mine were a father and son who died with their arms around each other.

"The old-timers used to say, 'some day this one is gonna blow'," he recalled. "But us younger guys didn't think nothin' of it."

The son of Austrian immigrants, Kastelitz was 33 at the time of the explosion. He had been mining for 10 years, tracing the footsteps of his father, who had been killed in the same mine nine years earlier when he was crushed by a rock. After the Smith Mine explosion, Kastelitz went back to work in the mine and worked there until it closed four years later.

"I went to the mines because there were no other jobs," he said. But despite the apparent misery and perpetual danger of underground mining, Kastelitz said both he and his father liked the work. "The mine was like home to my dad," he said. "He'd just as soon be in the mine as at home." It was the same

MICHAEL CRUMMETT

for Kastelitz, who remembers the camaraderie that developed among his co-workers. "There were seven men to a crew, and we always worked with the same crew," he said. "We talked things out every day and got pretty tight."

It has been said that mining gets into a man's blood and that once a miner, always a miner. John Kastelitz is representative of a wave of immigrant families who settled the mining camps of Montana when he said, "If I had to choose again, I would probably choose coal mining. It was a good job."

Not even Finn Day at Red Lodge's annual Festival of Nations can draw sisters Ellen and Miriam Lahti away from their household chores. Such is the lot of the characteristically hardworking Finns.

Two of 12 children born to Finnish immigrants, Miriam and Ellen left school in their early teens to go to work. After a serious injury ended his mining career, their father took up ranching. Family members worked on the ranch and picked up odd jobs in town to make ends meet. Ellen enrolled in a New Deal program called the National Youth Administration and learned how to sew. "We were paid $14 a month and, believe me, that sounded like a million bucks," she said. To this day, people from as far away as Billings bring their sewing to her.

From the day their folks arrived in America, life was a struggle, according to Ellen, but they never looked back. Finland was under Russian rule at the time, and they had no desire to

JOHN REDDY

Right: Homemade lefse is just one of the Old World treats to be found at the annual Red Lodge Festival of Nations.
Below: Red Lodge sisters Miriam and Ellen Lahti are characteristically hard-working Finns.

Facing page, top: Retired coal miner John Kastelitz remembers Bearcreek's Smith Mine Disaster of 1943 as if it happened yesterday.
Bottom: Site of the Smith Mine Disaster near Red Lodge.

MICHAEL CRUMMETT PHOTOS

return because "things were worse over there." One of Ellen's most vivid memories of her father is of him removing his hat whenever the American flag passed by during the annual Fourth of July parade. Like so many immigrants, the Lahtis abandoned their homeland and pledged allegiance to America.

Ellen and Miriam still speak Finnish with one another occasionally "just to make sure we don't lose it." But like their folks, they don't look back. "Some of our background we'd just as soon forget because the times were so tough," said Ellen.

In a state known for its friendly people, Eddie McCarthy is a standout. The retired Anaconda mail carrier treasures old friends as if they were his only friends and cultivates new friends every day. Eddie can't help it; he's Irish.

For 41 years, he gathered up friends on his mail route. The day he retired, the whole community showed up at his last stop on Tammany Street to give him a champagne send-off.

Every year on the Sunday before St. Patrick's Day, Eddie and his wife, Bea, host one of the largest private parties in Montana. What started in 1965 as a small reception for family and friends has become *the place* in Southwestern Montana to kick off the week of St. Patrick's Day. Depending on the weather, the McCarthys expect anywhere from 500 to 1,000 Irish and friends of Irish to show up at their front door.

Bea, a school teacher and member of the Montana Board of Regents, starts baking and freezing cakes about a month beforehand. Eddie starts planning next year's party the day after the last one, picking up a bottle or two of "party beverages" every couple of weeks so there will be plenty on hand when his shamrock-shaped "Advent calendar" announces that St. Patrick's Day is only a week away.

"It is something great," Eddie said of the party. "I really enjoy having these people around." He discourages people from bringing food because "it is just something I want to do for the community." He recalled all the times the folks on his mail route invited him in for coffee and treats. Mostly they just wanted to talk. "The Irish seem to like to get together and talk," he said unnecessarily.

Life has been good to Eddie McCarthy because he has made it that way. While some people would tire of delivering mail day in and day out for 40 years, Eddie describes it as the highlight of his life. "I got to meet so many people," he said of his beloved walking route. While some people quit living when they quit working, Eddie thrives on retirement. It gives him that much more time with his family and friends. Eddie attributes his bright spirit to his folks—"I never heard them fight"—and he has made a point of passing it along to his five kids: "I've always told them it doesn't cost any more to smile."

Anacondan Eddie McCarthy pauses at the entrance to his basement, where Irish and friends of Irish are always welcome.

It is not surprising to Ding K. Tam that nearly every Montana town of any size has a Chinese restaurant. People like Chinese food simply because it is good. "Chinese food is more healthy, more vegetable, more digestible," said Tam, who is better known as Danny Wong in Butte, where he presides over a popular noodle parlor called the Pekin Cafe.

Opened in 1916 by his great uncle, the second-floor walk-up is an uptown institution. Diners are drawn as much by the cozy atmosphere of its curtained booths as they are by the always-dependable pork noodles and boiled won ton.

Like so many Chinese immigrants, Tam's ancestors followed the mining industry to Butte prior to the turn of the century. From the window of his restaurant, Tam can point to the Toyota car lot where his great-great-grandfather's laundry business was located. In 1948, Tam emigrated from Canton, China to be with his grandfather, who worked as a doctor and ran a casino business in the same building that houses the restaurant. He started working at the restaurant in 1952.

Tam has returned many times to his homeland to visit his family and pay his respects to deceased elders, but Butte is his home. He will not say when or why he took on a second name, but it was undoubtedly a business decision. "Everyone knows me as Wong," he said, laughing. "Wong is like Sullivan in Butte."

Ding K. Tam, aka Danny Wong, puts out 70 pounds of marinated pork loin a day at his popular uptown Butte noodle parlor.

The mining city has changed a lot since the days when workers put in three shifts on the hill and the noodle parlor did its best business after 2 a.m., but even today, he said, "our business is always steady." He still enjoys cooking, but he has his hands full managing a kitchen that puts out 70 pounds of marinated pork loin and 100 pounds of homemade wonton wrappers a day.

Right: *Indian firefighters like this Northern Cheyenne got a good work out during the record fire season of 1988.*
Below: *Basque sheepman Fred Itcaina of Dodson with new lamb.*
Bottom: *John Sallaberry and Fred Itcaina assess the day's work by counting tails.*

MICHAEL CRUMMETT PHOTOS BOTH PAGES

Most would say the climate and soil of the lower Yellowstone River Valley make the area from Columbus to Sidney such good sugar beet country. But, according to one of the valley's leading growers, it is also the interest people take in growing the crop. In other words, according to Ishmael "Babe" Yost, "it is the people." And the people, for the most part, are Russian Germans who have been growing beets for generations, first in Germany, then in the Volga River Valley of Russia and now in America.

Babe and Mary Yost are descendants of the wave of German immigrants who arrived in America before World War I. Those who migrated first to Russia in search of land before seeking freedom and economic opportunity in America were industrious farm people who worked only a few years as beet laborers before they laid down their hoes and bought their own farms. Like the other Russian Germans who settled in the Yellowstone Valley, Babe and Mary's families arrived shortly after the founding of the Billings sugar factory.

It was his commitment to his fellow producers, coupled with his ability to get along with the management of the Great Western Sugar Company, that propelled Babe Yost into a position of leadership among Montana's beet growers. So tenacious and skillful was he in contract negotiations that he was re-elected president of the Mountain States Beet Growers Marketing Association for 27 years.

Dozens of plaques and certificates bear witness to his distinguished farm career and service to numerous civic organizations. But what gives him the most pleasure these days are the memories of well-fought contests and show-downs between him and the management of the sugar company, especially during the mid- to late 1970s, when it was owned by the Hunt brothers of Texas.

MICHAEL CRUMMETT PHOTOS BOTH PAGES

Leah Cole, *rancher, Garfield County:*
"I've been to the Midwest, where she's all flat and in squares. Now, that's flat."

"My pattern has always been to do what you can for the other guy," he said of his lifelong effort to achieve fair prices for his fellow producers. "For three years, I fought for my belief that each grower should be paid for his individual sugar content instead of receiving an average payment based on all the states' producers."

Babe and Mary Yost are Americans first, but the Old Country is still perceptible in their conversation and lifestyle. "Our parents would have felt shunned and hurt if we had neglected our past," said Babe. "They loved this country but felt strongly that our background should be recognized."

Retired sugar beet growers "Babe" and Mary Yost were leaders in their industry.

The mill at Libby has provided a good living for two generations of Nelsons but the work has changed dramatically since 1948, when Frank Nelson first went to work for the J. Neils Lumber Company. Like other wood products plants in Western Montana, the mill, now owned by Champion International, has made deep reductions in its labor force in an industry-wide move toward mechanization.

Joel Nelson, who works as a log procurement administrator for Champion, feels he was lucky to find work in his hometown after graduating from the University of Montana School of Forestry in 1976. He thinks he'll be even luckier to stay. "My personal goal has been to make myself as flexible and presentable as possible," he said. "I enjoy living in Libby, Montana, but I have to face the fact that I may not always be here." When he first went to work at the mill, he joined a workforce of 1,100; today, he is one of about 650 workers at the mill.

The grandson of Norwegian and Swedish immigrants, Joel is at home in the woods of Lincoln County. Changes in the industry, however, are forcing him to become more active in the public arena. Criticism of forest management practices, a dwindling supply of old-growth timber on private lands, multiple appeals tying up timber sales on public lands and an unyielding debate over wilderness are issues Joel's dad never had to contend with.

"Loggers aren't real outspoken people," Joel said, "but they realize they have to get involved in these debates if they want to keep working." Joel believes there is a permanent place for loggers in the ecology of Western Montana. "I'm a biological forester," he said. "I understand that trees can be cut and trees will grow back."

An employee of a multinational corporation, Joel is less certain about his own future than that of his hometown. Regardless of the changes affecting the wood products industry, he is convinced that "there will always be a mill here because this is timber country."

From the patio deck of Jack and Ann Hirschy's Big Hole ranch, there is no shortage of natural attractions. To the east, through a mallard-filled sky, is a changing view of the West Pioneer range; to the west, the snow-flanked Bitterroots. In every direction, there is wildlife—sandhill cranes, Canada geese, raptors and, in season, moose and elk. The dominant attraction on the deck, however, is its man-made centerpiece—a 200-gallon copper kettle that serves as a reminder to Jack Hirschy of who he is and why he is there.

Nearly 100 years ago, in 1894, Jack's grandparents homesteaded the Big

MICHAEL CRUMMETT PHOTOS BOTH PAGES

Above: Harvesting sugar beets in Yellowstone County.
Inset: Ed Troutman operates a sugar beet dump station near Huntley.

Facing page: Champion International log procurement officer Joel Nelson feels he was lucky to find work in his hometown of Libby.

Hole Basin ranch. Swiss emigrants, they were dairy farmers and cheesemakers. "They made a living by selling butter and cheese to the miners in Butte and Anaconda," said Ann. "That's all they knew."

But the climate is not well suited to dairy farming, Jack explained, so it was not long before they learned how to raise beef cattle. The Hirschys have been raising cattle ever since.

"Cattle and hay," Jack amended.

Known as the "valley of 10,000 haystacks," the Big Hole looks like an agrarian landscape out of the past. Throughout the valley's 50-mile length and 15-mile width are haystacks piled high as houses. More distinct on the horizon are the beaverslide hay derricks that have been used to stack hay since they were invented by two Big Hole ranchers in 1907.

Hay grows wild in the Big Hole, contributing heavily to Beaverhead County's standing as the top cattle and hay producer in the state. At 6,500 feet, that is about all you can do with the valley.

We Montanans

"Mosquitoes and cold weather, that's what keeps this valley from developing," said Jack.

On one of April's first warm days, it is hard to imagine either. Calving is nearly finished. Irrigation (read "mosquitoes") is a month away. The grass is turning and the breeze is benign. A darkening western sky promises moisture, and that is a promise you can generally count on in the Big Hole, according to Jack. "We've never had a drought," he said. "We've had dry years, but we've never lost a hay crop due to drought."

It was a spring day much like this when Jack's grandparents arrived in the valley. It is no wonder they stayed. Nor is it surprising that Jack and Ann's grandchilden are also their neighbors. Over the past century, the Big Hole has produced millions of tons of hay and beef, and supported five generations of Hirschys.

Facing page: Middle Fork of the Flathead River, Glacier National Park.
Below: Ann and Jack Hirschy say it's the mosquitoes and cold weather that keep the Big Hole Valley from developing.

MICHAEL CRUMMETT

From the deck, Ann raised her eyes toward another incoming flight of mallards. "We don't take it for granted," she said.

Starting over again has not been easy for Montana's newest immigrants—the Hmong or "hill" people of Southeast Asia. But as it was for many of the immigrants who came before, life here is better than what they left behind. Their arrival in Montana, starting in 1976, was the latest in a tormented history of upheavals and migrations for the Hmong, who were pushed from their earliest homeland of southern China into North Vietnam, Laos and Thailand. Most of the Hmong who survived the Vietnam War were pushed once more out of Southeast Asia and settled in France, Australia and the United States. At the height of their settlement in Montana, 700 to 800 Hmong were living primarily in the Bitterroot Valley. Some moved to Billings but most moved on to more established Hmong communities in California, Minnesota, Wisconsin and Washington, leaving Montana with a small but stable population of about 300.

Over a period of three years during his late teens, Pao Moua lived in three different countries—Laos, Thailand and the United States. Since 1976, he has lived in Missoula where he manages the Iron Wok, a restaurant that features the cuisine of Southeast Asia. Co-owned by Pao's brother and a non-Asian Missoula family, the Iron Wok represents the integration of the Hmong into the Missoula community.

True to the Hmong experience, the process has been long and difficult. Although Montana churches and social agencies were active in finding homes and jobs for these refugees, the Hmong were not universally accepted by Montanans. "Montana is a big state but the people are so much alike, it was hard for them to accept us," said Pao. "Some of us were abused at first, and many left, but now is better."

So much better that Pao said he would be happy to stay. Besides the stability he and his family have found here, Pao enjoys "the nature, the fresh

Betty Steele, cowgirl, Malta:
"Even on the prairie, you never get all the way to the top or the bottom. There's always a higher hill or a deeper coulee."

JOHN REDDY

Right: *Hauling hay down U.S. 2 near Brockton.*
Below: *The view from the top of a beaverslide hay derrick.*

TOM DIETRICH

In the Big Hole Valley near Jackson.

air, the fishing and hunting" of Western Montana which, in many ways, resembles his homeland of Laos. "We hunted wild boar, deer, antelope and peacock," he said. The hunting experience is the same here but "there were more animals to hunt there."

Pao Moua is "proud to be here in America" and does not miss his homeland. "The way the superpowers play around with the smaller countries, it's pretty risky business," he said. "I would rather be over here."

MICHAEL CRUMMETT

Mao and Pao Moua in the Iron Wok, Missoula.

ETHNIC IS IN: MONTAN

MICHAEL CRUMMETT

Intertribal dance on Rocky Boy's Reservation.

Greeks love a good party, and in 1989 Missoula's small but active Greek community will invite the whole town to its third annual Greek festival, a party that runs two nights, featuring traditional Greek food and dance. For the ninth year, Anaconda's Croation community will gather on the Saturday before Ash Wednesday for Mesopust, a pre-Lenten celebration that features humorous skits, the music of tamburitza bands and the kielbasa and cabbage rolls of some very good Yugoslavian cooks. A Dutch dinner featuring old world treats like *kippen, roggebrood* and *saucijzebroodjes,* and the entertainment of *klompen* (wooden shoe) dancers, is in its 10th year at Churchill, near Bozeman.

Across Montana, the descendants of foreign-born immigrants are researching family histories and reviving Old Country traditions to expose ethnic roots that have been buried by at least two generations of active assimilation.

The linguists and anthropologists have a name for it. They call it the "third-generation return." We're in the midst of a predictable ethnic revival in Montana,

JOHN REDDY

Everyone is welcome at the St. Patrick's Day Parade in Butte, including a Scottish pipe band.

according to University of Montana (UM) language professor Tony Beltramo, who said it will subside as surely as it surfaced.

Beltramo has logged census statistics dating to 1910, which reveal that while the real numbers of people with a non-English mother tongue have been declining in Montana, the proportion of people willing to claim a non-English mother tongue has been rising. Roughly three generations after American immigrants began arriving in Montana, ethnicity is in vogue.

"My mother would turn over in her grave if she knew how we carry on," said a Helena woman with an active social network of Swedish family and friends who keep the "old ways" alive in their smorgasbord dinners and St. Lucia Day festivals. "She worked so hard at becoming an American, she rejected her Swedish homeland."

The same story can be heard over and over again throughout Montana. Such was the immigrant experience. John Kastelitz, a retired coal miner from Red Lodge, recalled his immigrant father telling the kids: "We're no longer Austrians; we're Americans now."

If they hadn't rejected their homeland by the time they reached Ellis Island, they were surely Americans after they had served their adopted country in war. Until 1947, services at the Manhattan Christian Re-

MICHAEL CRUMMETT PHOTOS

Above: *Dressed up for Crow Fair.*
Right: *El Paso Cafe concession crew at Billings' Cinco de Mayo festival.*

formed Church in Churchill were conducted in Dutch. "The war made Americans out of all of us," said Mary Swier-Bolhuis, a member of the Gallatin County Dutch community. "Once you're drafted, you're an American. When our men came home from the war, the language was dropped and services were in English from then on."

Language is one of the most visible indicators of ethnic identity. With few exceptions, Montana's immigrants abandoned their native tongue when they arrived in America and went to work. While many of them kept the language alive in their homes and ethnic neighborhoods, they insisted their children learn English. In fact, many immigrants learned English from their school-aged children.

"The exigencies of living on the frontier or working in the mine were more important than being Italian or Irish," said UM's Beltramo. "The job of recapturing an ancestral language today is the same as learning any foreign language, enhanced perhaps by the call of one's heritage. It is a matter of personal interest, not community need. So, a person is just as likely to devote the time to, say, rosemaling."

On at least two Indian reservations, revival of the language is, indeed, a community need, if not a crusade. Both the Blackfeet and Flathead Indians have learned a new technique for teaching their native language and are working with their elders to pass it on before it passes away.

"Each time an elder passes away, they take a little something with them," said Tony Incashola of the Flathead Culture Committee. "As they disappear, so does the language."

Incashola estimated that only 100 to 200 of the Flathead tribe's 6,000 enrolled members are fluent in their native language.

"Revival of our language is the highest priority of our culture committee," he said. "If there is no language, there is no culture. And if there is no culture, then we're no different from anyone else."

Right: *Crow artistry.*
Bottom: *Blackfeet Indian artist Neil Parsons utilizes traditional Northern Plains Indian symbol in a contemporary oil painting.*
Facing page, top: *Salish-Kootenai Indians on the Flathead Reservation are working hard to revive their native language before it disappears.*
Below: *A traditional Greek dance.*

MICHAEL CRUMMETT PHOTOS BOTH PAGES

2

LIFESTYLE IS A DRAW FOR NATIVES AND NEWCOMERS ALIKE

Mike Murphy, *outfitter, Musselshell:*

"I actually moved to Florida for three weeks. I was going to make a lot of money and be a yuppie. But I couldn't stay because I felt like I was living on an ant hill. We left Montana because we were going broke, but I knew I had to return."

Montana's early settlers would be amused to learn that those who followed a century later would choose this challenging land for something called "quality of life." From the homesteaders who literally lost their minds on the isolated, windblown plains of Eastern Montana to the copper and coal miners whose final reward for a life underground was an early death from silicosis, Montana hardly fulfilled the promise of a better life. Still they came, and still they come.

Montana continues to hold out the promise of something better, but these days it has more to do with affordable housing, good neighbors and uncrowded trout streams than it does with financial security or professional opportunity. Peace of mind and a reasonable pace of life rank high with Montana's newest pilgrims, who bring fresh perspective to a lifestyle most natives take for granted.

And what of the natives? What of the those who have called Montana home for two, three, four, even five generations? Many are carrying out the legacy left by their grandparents and great-grandparents on family farms and ranches. Many have left temporarily to try life on the "outside," only to return to the communities and families and friends—to the lifestyle—they couldn't find elsewhere. Many—too many, in the minds of most Montanans—have left the state permanently in pursuit of jobs and opportunities that simply do not exist here. Others have dreamed up ingenious ways to stay and make it pay.

Most are here by choice, enjoying a lifestyle that eludes most other Americans.

In Arnold Bolle's mind, it is no coincidence that America's first national park lies on

RICK GRAETZ

PAT O'HARA

Above: Montanans treasure scenes like this one in Glacier National Park.
Facing page: Montana's newest pilgrims seek something called quality of life.

the southern border of Montana or that the nation's Wild and Scenic River system rises in the forks of the Flathead River. Milestones in the nation's conservation history, both originated as ideas of visionary Montanans. Nor is it surprising to Bolle that the American wilderness movement has roots in Montana, where pioneer forester and conservationist Bob Marshall spent much of his short life.

Bolle, the retired dean of the University of Montana (UM) School of Forestry, believes Montana attracts the kind of people who feel strongly about the preservation of public lands. More important, it attracts the kind of people who can get the job done.

"Every Montanan who comes here wants to keep it just the way it was when he got here," he said with a laugh, including himself in the accusation. Bolle came to Montana more than 50 years ago as a forestry student. A position with the U.S. Soil Conservation Service and a mid-career opportunity to study at Harvard University took him away for a while but in 1955 he returned to the forestry school, this time as a professor.

During the time he served as dean, from 1962 to 1972, the UM School of Forestry came to be known as the place to learn about a new concept called "multiple use." Unlike other forestry schools in the West that narrowed their focus to timber production, range or watershed management, the UM forestry school developed strong components in the fields of recreation management and wildlife biology.

During the same period, Bolle became a national leader in forest management policy after chairing a congressional study of U.S. Forest Service clear-cutting practices on the Bitterroot National Forest. The study, requested by the late U.S. Senator Lee Metcalf, focused on one forest but laid the groundwork for a national overhaul of forest service policy. Known as the Bolle Report, it led to passage in 1976 of the National Forest Management Act. Bolle is proud of his part in the legislative process but credits another conservation giant, Lee Metcalf, with getting the job done.

"There was a growing perception that the Forest Service was absorbed totally with timber production," he recalled. "The idea behind the act is that public forests are different from private forests and that sustained yield applies to all forest products— water, wildlife, recreation and timber."

Arnold Bolle, retired dean of the UM School of Forestry, believes Montana attracts people who feel strongly about preservation of public lands and "get the job done."

As a professor, Bolle taught his students to be well rounded people and active, informed citizens as well as good foresters. As dean, his influence extended from the Missoula campus to the halls of Congress. In retirement, he has been an effective wilderness proponent. A respected elder in Montana's conservation community, Bolle has taken his place in the tradition that drew him to Montana in the first place.

The first day Jerry Wells was in Montana, he went out to the Gallatin River and caught a three-pound brown trout. That was in 1972. He had moved here to study fish-and-wildlife management at Montana State University. "That was it for me," he said roughly two decades later. "There was never a question that I would stay, just a question of what I would do."

Wells still lives in Bozeman, but his job has cut seriously into his fishing time. As regional fisheries manager for the Montana Department of Fish, Wildlife and Parks, he is responsible for Southwestern Montana's wild trout fishery—the centerpiece of a resource that generates nearly $100 million a year in sportsmen's expenditures.

Montana's fishery resource is indisputably world-class. But it did not happen by accident. "The people who live in this state have made our success possible," said Wells as he ticked off a string of legislative victories that, over the years, have built a solid framework for the conservation and protection of Montana's water resources. But credit also must go to Wells and the department's other biologists and managers, many of whom have moved

Fisheries manager Jerry Wells says his job has little to do with biology. "I work with people."

Autumn looks kindly on Morgan Creek, between Glendive and Sidney.

here from outside the state. "When people have seen things destroyed elsewhere, they work harder to protect something pristine and wonderful in Montana," said the former Denver resident.

Wells has watched his work change dramatically over the years. As stream conditions and habitat have improved, so has the fishing. In turn, numbers of fishermen and their value to the state's economy have grown. Today, the fieldwork that Wells was trained for has little relevance to the day-to-day job of managing this increasingly valuable resource.

"My work has very little to do with biology," said Wells as he sandwiched an interview between meetings and phone calls. "I work with people." He sees the job getting tougher as the department's emphasis evolves from the quality of the fishery to the quality of the fishing experience. Growing numbers of fishermen, the carrying capacity of Montana's rivers and streams, and the varying types and preferences of anglers are just some of the problems he faces.

Life can be frustrating for a biologist who finds himself, more and more, doing the work of a sociologist. But for Jerry Wells, just knowing there are more three-pound browns out there now than there were in 1972 makes it all worthwhile.

In a state that chronically laments the exportation of its kids to out-of-state jobs, one occupation begs for good help. Cowboys for hire Doug Wall of Miles City and Betty Steele of Malta have more work than they can handle. Ridin' is their business, and when they're not movin' cows, sortin' cows, brandin' cows, breakin' horses, buyin' and sellin' horses or shoein' horses, chances are they're doin' what they love best and that's rodeoin'.

"I don't ever have to worry about a job; someone's always on the phone lookin' for a rider," Betty said on a sub-zero February day between breaking someone's colt and filling in at the local veterinary clinic. "I take time off for rodeos but I could be busy every day of the year."

Betty grew up on a ranch outside of Lewistown and started riding at a young age. In high school, she caught rodeo fever and started riding and breaking horses for other people in order to finance her new passion. She has a well stocked belt buckle collection, one that grows each year when she competes in the International Feedlot Cowboys Association Rodeo. In 1987, she won both mixed roping and barrels at the association's regional event in Billings.

Doug got started the same way, competing in his first rodeo at age 14. He turned professional in 1962 and made his living as a saddle bronc and bareback rider for 23 years. He has competed in rodeos throughout the country, but his favorite is still the Miles City Buckin' Horse Sale, where he now works as a "pickup man," picking up riders at the end of their ride and delivering horses to the cool-down area. He retired from competition in 1980 "'bout the time I got to the point I couldn't beat anybody anymore, so I quit," he grinned.

But he is far from retirement age as a cowboy. All those busted

Cowboys-for-hire Doug Wall and Betty Steele could work every day of the year, but they take time out for rodeos.

Top: *After roping all day, there's time for a little more practice.*
Above: *Cowboy Tom Hagwood keeps watch on a calf during branding at the Padlock Ranch, southeast of Hardin.*
Right: *Betty Steele is known on the rodeo circuit as an ace roper.*

ankles and shoulders paid off in the long run. He may work for someone else, but the job is always on his terms: "I get to ride. That's what I like to do. I'm not one for drivin' tractor or buildin' fence."

Doug estimated there are at least 100 cowboys making a living as "hands" in the Miles City area and predicts the work will hold out "as long as there are big ranches in Montana."

Life could have taken Paul Ringling down several paths but he is glad he followed the one that led to Carter County. He has engaged in several ventures, but mostly, Paul Ringling is a cowman, and a good one.

Born into the circus family, Paul had the right connections to go off and join the circus at a young age. For four years, he toured the country, selling tickets, setting up and tearing down equipment and promoting the Ringling Brothers Circus. From there, he went into military service and spent another two-and-a-half years overseas. But he never lost his love of the ranch he grew up on near White Sulphur Springs and returned home to manage it in 1946.

Over the years, Paul has exhibited one of the traits that brought his Great Uncle John to Montana in the first place. "He saw Montana as a place where he could make some money on land deals," Paul said of John Ringling, one of the original five brothers who started the circus. John had deals "going all over the country," according to Paul, but Montana was his base of operation.

Similarly, Paul has not been content merely to sell cattle. Buying and selling ranches, plus a lifelong interest in politics, have been part of a formula that keeps life interesting for Paul and Althea Ringling. Between ranching operations in Meagher and Carter counties, they owned a ranch in Sweet Grass County, south of the Crazy Mountains. "We were looking for a ranch in Montana that we thought would work, a ranch that a cow would pay for," Paul said of their decision to leave the Crazies and buy a ranch in Carter County. "We looked at a place in Arizona but we no sooner got down there to look at it than we stepped on the gas," he said. "My idea is that scrub cedars and cattle don't go together."

Carter County, by contrast, is "good grass country," in Ringling's opinion. It is good people country, too. "We have good friends here," Paul said. "But ranch people aren't that different. We've had good ranch neighbors everywhere we've been."

Dr. Paul Lauren has the best of both worlds, and he knows it. He assumed he would pay professionally for the personal choice he made when he left Stanford University for a faculty position at the University of Montana (UM) in 1974. Little did he know at the time that he was positioning himself for the professional opportunity of a lifetime.

As director of UM's new Maureen and Mike Mansfield Center, Dr. Lauren glowed when he said: "There is nothing I could have done to plan for this." In fact, he was perfectly suited for the job. A history professor who specialized in international affairs and ethics, Dr. Lauren was the logical choice to head the Mansfield Center, which opened in 1986 to provide educational opportunities in the fields of Asian studies and ethics in government. In addition to its undergraduate and graduate curriculum, the center

Facing page: Buckling up at the annual Miles City Bucking Horse Sale.
Below: Rancher Paul Ringling chose Carter County because it is "good grass country."

Bob Kelly, *business consultant, Missoula:*
"In my work with resource issues over the years, I've noticed that the more polarized the individual leaders of the various interest groups are, the more likely they are to be transplants from other states."

Right: Salish-Kootenai Indians gathered on the University of Montana campus in 1987 to commemorate the Hellgate Treaty of 1855.
Below: Dr. Paul Lauren is director of the University of Montana's Maureen and Mike Mansfield Center. He says that Montanans make "an indelibly positive impression on visitors, especially foreigners."

sponsors student and faculty exchange programs in China and Japan and an annual conference that brings world leaders in business and government to the Missoula campus.

It is in this mix of Montanans with foreign dignitaries that Dr. Lauren has fully recognized the wisdom of his decision to leave the academic fast track of Stanford for the pace and the people of Montana. "Montanans make an indelibly positive impression on visitors, especially foreigners," he said. "Visitors feel comfortable and safe here. They like the values they find here. And they can't believe Montana is as pretty or as big as it is, or that the people are as friendly as they are."

He has as much to say for his students as he does for his contemporaries. "The bright students at UM are every bit as smart as the bright students at Stanford; it's just that at Stanford, they're all bright," he said. "The biggest difference is that students here are so incredibly honest and unpretentious. If they

We Montanans

Maureen O'Boyle, *co-founder, Naughty Pines Chicken Farm, Whitefish:*

"Montana needs its natives who understand the heritage of the state, but we also need the experience of the outside world to make Montana better."

Right: *Harvesting seed potatoes at Starkel Farms, near Ronan, in the Mission Valley.*
Below: *Organic-chicken farmers (left to right) Robin Riley, Thelma Lee and Maureen O'Boyle barely can keep up with the demand for their product.*

MICHAEL CRUMMETT PHOTOS

TOM DIETRICH

get a 'C', they take responsibility for it rather than trying to bully the professor into raising their grade."

Dr. Lauren goes on and on about the virtues of Montana, but he is aware of its drawbacks. It is his observation that "the parochialism of this state" is its downside. "I'd like to make a small contribution to educating Montanans on public affairs in the U.S. and the world," he said. "We're not competing with Stanford. We're trying to do something for Montana that brings credit to Mike and Maureen Mansfield."

Chrys Landrigan insists that the people who know her well would agree that her new lifestyle as owner of the Polebridge Mercantile is more characteristic of her personality than the career she left behind in New York City. Before moving to Montana, Landrigan put in 13 years as an office manager and auction organizer for Sotheby's, the world's largest auction gallery. Shortly after she left her job, Sotheby's sold an original Van Gogh painting for $53 million. "My friends told me they needed wheelbarrows to haul their commissions to the bank," she said. Without a trace of regret, she added, "Now I'm selling cans of Oly and Snickers bars."

MICHAEL CRUMMETT

Above: *Chrys Landrigan worked in New York City as an auction organizer for Sotheby's before she bought the Polebridge Mercantile.* **Below:** *Missoula consultant Bob Kelly is working to add value to Montana's raw materials.*

Far from a premeditated move, her acquisition of the Merc was an accident. After a few brief trips from New York to visit friends in Polebridge, she found herself becoming attached to the area and was worried when she learned the combination general store, gas station, post office and weather station was for sale. "I was afraid some awful person—like a New Yorker—would buy it," she said, "so I decided to buy it myself."

That was in 1987, and Manhattan is but a memory. "I enjoyed New York very much, but Polebridge is home," she said.

Besides some of the obvious advantages Montana has over Manhattan, Landrigan appreciates the sense of personal responsibility she has regained since leaving the city. "Out here, you're responsible for yourself, and you can get results very quickly," she explained. "If you're cold, you can put more wood on the fire; in the city, if your apartment is freezing, you can call the landlord, and if you're lucky, you'll get some relief in three days. If someone double-parks in front of your car, you can be stuck for hours."

JOHN REDDY

Facing page: *Old farmstead along the North Fork of the Flathead River, north of Polebridge.*

For years, Montanans have been wringing their hands about the need to add value to the state's raw materials before they leave the state. Bob Kelly has decided to stick around and try to do something about it. The founder of a new Missoula business called Intertec, Kelly described his role as the "eyes and ears" of Montana businesspeople who are "so busy minding the store, they don't have the luxury of time to look beyond their immediate horizon."

We Montanans

The kind of vision Kelly is talking about requires not only time but optimism. On good days, he can see Montana refining the rare and precious metals that are now leaving the state in boxcars. But right now, he is concentrating on expanding the market for Montana timber products. "Traditionally, the wood products industry in Montana has been geared to the housing market," he said. "There is a lot of high-quality timber leaving the state that would have higher value as cut stock, ready to assemble, for doors, windows and furniture."

Kelly has traveled around the country and in Europe to study the technology being used by other manufacturers to determine whether it can be applied in Montana. He is also looking for financing to help capitalize Montana enterprises. He thinks the state's small mills and manufacturers are well suited to new technology because they are more flexible and adaptable to change than large corporations.

A former environmental specialist for the Atlantic Richfield Company and public relations officer for Champion International, Kelly knows the resource industry in Montana. The son of an Anaconda smelter worker and grandson of a Butte miner, he also knows the bitter history of Montana's dominance by out-of-state corporations. He grew up on stories about the Anaconda Company, like the one his dad, Bob "Shipwreck" Kelly tells: "They even told the men how to vote, and if they didn't vote right, they got the red card."

Hence his desire to make Montana more self-reliant. "Being a native, I see a lot of opportunities that this state has failed to capitalize on," Kelly said. "It's not going to happen unless some of us stay around and make it happen."

MICHAEL CRUMMETT

Janet and Jerry Fenger say farming is a gamble but they stay with it because "it's a good life."

It was Labor Day weekend 1987. School already had started in Chester, and the weather was getting more unpredictable by the day. One of the hoses on their Massey had busted, and they waited four days for the new part to reach Great Falls. Unseasonable summer rains had already delayed the harvest. The wheat was lodging and slow to pick up. Some of it already had been lost to hail, some to sawflies. But Jerry and Janet Fenger were optimistic. Their crop looked good, and the moisture they were battling this year would produce an even better crop next year.

Next year will be better. If they did not believe it, the Fengers and many other farmers and ranchers would be out of the business in a minute. Between the weather and the world markets for grain and livestock, agriculture makes Las Vegas look like a conservative investment.

TOM DIETRICH

Right: *Fields of corn and wheat in the Little Bighorn Valley.*
Below: *Wheat field near Ulm.*

JOHN REDDY

"I won't gamble my money on machines or the lottery, but I will gamble on farming," said Janet Fenger. "It's a good life."

Located about 15 miles northwest of Chester, just south of the Sweet Grass Hills, the Fengers are masters of their own empire—a business and a piece of ground they bought from Jerry's folks and hope to pass on to their kids. They live and work according to the seasons. The hours are long and the pay is unpredictable. But the rewards are many: the satisfaction of harvest, a stolen afternoon float on the Marias

River, the fall hunt, an occasional trip to Great Falls for a concert, three well adjusted kids and a firm sense, among all five, of who they are and what it is all about.

Along about November, you start seeing them by the hundreds on Interstate 15 and Interstate 94. RV's and "5th-wheelers" with Montana plates, heading south as if in formation. Montana's "snowbirds" are ditching the north country for the more benign climates of Phoenix, Mesa, San Diego and Palm Springs. For a growing number of Montanans, a trailer court or condominium down south has solved the chronic problem of winter in Montana.

In West Yellowstone, where annual snowfall averages 200 inches and national-low temperatures give the whole state a bad rap, a growing year-round population is gearing up for its favorite season. Summer crowds are gone and neighbors are getting reacquainted. "We all wave good-bye to one another on Memorial Day, and say hello again about Halloween," said Jan Dunbar, a high school English teacher and librarian.

Playing host to a floating population of well over 10,000 tourists in the summer, West Yellowstone shrinks back down to 800 in the winter. When Jan and her husband, Cal, first moved to West Yellowstone in 1961, the year-round population was only 360. Cal, a local businessman and city council member since 1971, attributes the growth and stability of the community to one factor: the snowmobile.

A fly fisherman by summer and skier by winter, Cal Dunbar can't say enough good things about snowmobiles: "They completely changed West Yellowstone by creating a winter economy. Families started moving to town, making it possible for West Yellowstone to have its own high school. Next came the bank, then a medical clinic."

While Cal has been a key player in the campaign to make West Yellowstone "the snowmobile capital of the world," it was the summer season and, specifically, the trout fishing that originally drew the Dunbars from a

MICHAEL REAGAN PHOTO, COURTESY TURNER BROADCASTING SYSTEM

Above: *Cal Dunbar, at left, enjoys swapping stories with fishing partner Bud Lilly.*
Below: *During the summer, Cal Dunbar reserves Wednesdays for fishing; during the winter Wednesdays are spent skiing at Big Sky.*

RICK GRAETZ

RONALD J. GLOVAN

TIM CHRISTIE

JOHN REDDY

Above: *It's never too soon to learn how to ski in Montana.*
Top: *Winter covers Montana with snow and silence.*
Right: *For many Montanans, the fishing season never ends.*

Dr. Larry Johnson started his laser-diode instrumentation business in Bozeman because he can be hiking or skiing within an hour of town.

MICHAEL CRUMMETT

Sharon Howe, *fundraiser, Helena:*

"When I was living in Pennsylvania, I got out of the habit of looking at people's faces. No one actually looks into people's faces in large cities. When I moved back, I was offended at first when people looked me in the eye. It seemed obtrusive. Now, I catch myself at a restaurant in Milwaukee or some other large city looking around to see if I know anyone."

corporate lifestyle in the San Francisco Bay area to Montana. Cal jokes that he married Jan because her family had a summer cabin on Hebgen Lake, and she retorts with the observation that Cal fishes "as if every day is his last."

"I'm interested in time allocation for sport," he said. "Day in and day out, there's always something feeding on the Madison, and I'm in the right place to take advantage of it."

Dr. Larry Johnson had several criteria when he was scouting a location for his new laser-diode instrumentation business. He and his wife wanted to live in a small city in the Rockies. For his business, he needed reliable air transportation, a university and a technical community. Above all, the location had to meet his "one-hour" rule: "If I can get in a car and be skiing or hiking within an hour, I'll do it frequently," said the young entrepreneur. "If it takes more than an hour, I won't do it."

A business trip brought Dr. Johnson to Bozeman on a brilliant, blue-and-white winter day in 1986, and he has been there ever since. That year, he opened ILX Lightwave, one of those exotic, new businesses that spun out of the laser technology boom. If Dr. Johnson is enthusiastic about his new Montana home, he is wild about laser diodes: "I fell in love with them as a technology and could easily see they would change laser technology dramatically." That was when he was heading a fiber-optic research team for a large company in Minnesota. Dissatisfied with the equipment that was available to his team of scientists, he saw a need and decided to carve out a niche in the instrumentation market. "We are the world leader right now, but it's a small market," he said. "Our strategy is to establish a leadership position and hang onto it."

"We" is a small group of about 20 employees at ILX who design and manufacture the instruments for laboratories that use laser diodes to create new products. Fiber optic telecommunications and compact disc players are two examples of what Dr. Johnson describes as the "laser-diode revolution." While it is difficult to foresee the impact of a new technology "when you're on the ground floor," he is convinced that the impact of laser diodes will be no less dramatic than that of the transistor, the integrated circuit or the microcomputer.

Can Montana provide an environment that nurtures this kind of industry? Dr. Johnson thinks so, or he would not be here. But he qualifies his enthusiasm with some of the obstacles he has already encountered: a lack of investors willing to finance new businesses, and difficulty in recruiting professional engineers and technicians to Montana. On a more subtle level, he expressed a keen understanding of the state for having been here such a short time: "Montanans struggle with growth. They're glad to see us, but they worry about the 'Denverization' of their community. Montana has been exploited by business, and its people are skeptical of new business. I can feel that undercurrent."

Hindrances, yes; roadblocks, no. Surrounded by large, scenic photos of Montana and dressed casually in jeans and a sweater, Dr. Johnson is in love with Montana and determined to make it work.

JOHN REDDY

Above: *Canoeing on Bowman Lake, Glacier National Park.*
Left: *Southwestern Montana's Madison River draws anglers from all over the world.*

TOM DIETRICH

*Community activist and heart
surgeon Dr. Hewes Agnew
chose Billings because he wanted
to live in a town "where a person
might make a difference."*

MICHAEL CRUMMETT

*Butte native and business
consultant Dennis Winters has
compassion for the underdog,
and the underdog, as he sees it,
is Montana. He and his wife,
Michelle LeFurge, formed the
Montana Market Development
Company to help Montana
producers develop better-paying
markets.*

JOHN REDDY

T o possess the ability to routinely save and extend people's lives would provide plenty of stimulation and self-satisfaction for most people. But the heroics of cardiac surgery are just part of a fulfilling life for Dr. Hewes Agnew, one of Billings' four heart surgeons.

Granted, it is a big part. Performing an average of 240 heart bypass surgeries a year, each one lasting four to five hours, plus post-operative care, Dr. Agnew has devoted himself to an intense, demanding profession. It is not like his earlier days as a general and thoracic surgeon when "a good week was a gall bladder, a stomach, a hernia and a couple of hearts." He enjoyed the diversity but recognizes it as a luxury. "You just can't do it that way any longer," he said. "Heart surgery requires a commitment of time."

Still, he has time at the end of the day for his family and a calendar of commitments that have nothing to do with medicine. As chairman of the fund drive for the Alberta Bair Theater, Dr. Agnew was the push behind a campaign that raised $5 million to open one of Montana's newest and largest performing arts facilities. Before that, he served as a member and president of the Billings School Board, president of the Billings Chamber of Commerce and a member of the Billings Local Government Study Commission.

The trick, he said, is to get involved in groups that meet late in the afternoon or in the evening. "And it's important to become president," he added, "so that you can influence the schedule."

Dr. Agnew has never regarded his role in civic affairs as burdensome. For him, it is therapeutic. "You meet a whole different cast of characters," he said, "and it gets your mind off things at work. It's been great fun."

A native of St. Louis, Missouri and a graduate of Princeton University and Johns Hopkins University, Dr. Agnew moved to Montana in 1972 when he joined the staff of the Billings Clinic. He chose Billings because he wanted to live in a town "where a person might make a difference."

M ost "Buttians" will tell you that growing up in Butte gave them an edge. A strong sense of belonging gave them the kind of self-confidence that goes a long way in the world of hard knocks. As one of the natives put it: "When you fell down, there was a good chance someone would come along and kick you in the ass, then give you a hug. That's why we go out in the world so cocky."

A more subtle source of strength lies in Butte's ethnic diversity. At one time, as many as 50 nationalities lived together in Butte. Kids growing up in that atmosphere learned tolerance at an early age and were comfortable with people who were "different." Many grew up speaking two languages at home. Here is how the cosmopolitan city of Butte launched two of its own.

Dennis Winters has spent most of his life outside of Butte, traveling and working in faraway places like Malaysia, Saudi

LOUIS PSIHOYOS

Dennis Winters believes Montana's ranchers are getting "street cleaners' wages for Ph.D. expertise."

Arabia and Europe. From 1976 to 1986, he and his wife, Michelle LeFurge, were political consultants to the Saudi government, working primarily with the minister of planning in his dealings with the U.S. government.

Now, they're in Butte, working together as the Montana Market Development Company on what may well be their most challenging venture: trying to persuade Montana producers to abandon their independence long enough to market cooperatively.

"We've been harvested and extracted for so long, we think only in terms of the next paycheck or the annual check from the grain elevator," said Winters. He should know. The son of a Butte miner, he still remembers the day his dad explained to the family that there would not be any money coming in because the miners had voted to strike. From Butte he went to Chicago, where he worked with the Reverend Jesse Jackson to organize boycotts against businesses that did not employ blacks or market their products. Next, he went to North Dakota, where he did similar work with Indian groups. Dennis

Winters has compassion for the underdog, and the underdog, as he sees it today, is Montana.

"The day is past that we can depend on others to market our richness," he said. "To the extent that we rely on others, we will continue to export our kids and our capital."

Winters has taken a special interest in Montana's farm and livestock producers who, in his opinion, are vastly underpaid. "Montana's ranchers are getting street cleaners' wages for Ph.D. expertise," he said bluntly. He hopes to build a bloc of producers who will work together to develop markets that will compensate producers for the quality and expertise they are selling.

"I'm like the obstetrician who came to town," he said. "Unless there are some very intense relationships, the obstetrician has no future. In this case, unless Montanans are willing to take some risks together, the future will be stillborn."

Carol Williams grew up as Carol Griffith in Butte, the daughter of a Cornish-Welsh grocery store owner and popular, two-term mayor. A part of Butte's speed-skating tradition, she was sidelined by a knee injury in 1961, but went on to coach speed skating during her first two years of college at Montana Tech. Some of her fondest memories of Butte are the weekends, when "the big thing to do was to go to Meaderville for a great Italian dinner," or the Christmas and New Year's celebrations that lasted two months. "After our own celebrations, we had Serbian Christmas in January and finished up with the Chinese New Year in February," she said.

Carol Williams is putting her Butte background to work trying to build friendships between the people of the United States and the Soviet Union.

PHOTO COURTESY CAROL WILLIAMS

Now living in Washington, D.C., with her husband, Congressman Pat Williams, Carol is still celebrating people's differences but her focus has shifted from hometown neighborhoods to U.S.-Soviet relations. A founding member of Peace Links, a national women's group opposed to nuclear arms, she is putting her Butte background to work trying to build friendships between the people of the United States and the Soviet Union. She has traveled in Russia as part of a Peace Links delegation and worked with Soviet delegations visiting America. On a good day back home in Montana, she will speak to half a dozen grade school classes, telling them about her experiences with the Soviet people and answering questions like: "How long do the kids go to school?" and "Who is their favorite rock group?"

"I grew up around people who were different," she said. "So it seemed natural for me to get involved in this kind of work in Washington—to get people to understand their cultural differences and be more tolerant of one another."

If you've ever been on a transcontinental flight from the East Coast to Seattle when the pilot starts raving about Montana as you fly over the Northern Rockies, chances are you were flying with Larry Ashcraft or another one of the estimated 50 commercial airline pilots who live in Montana and commute to work all over the globe.

Ashcraft, who grew up in Helena and now lives near Bigfork, said flying is a good job for a Montanan because "you can name where you want to live." The downside is that it takes a long time to commute to work from Montana.

DEAN SAUSKOJUS

Sprinkler irrigation has redefined the rural Montana skyline.

In his case, he spends two days a month just getting to and from TWA headquarters in St. Louis. "If I started analyzing how much time I waste when I could be with my family, I'd get depressed," he said. "I've talked to the family about moving, but they say, 'no way'."

Like most pilots, Ashcraft started dreaming about flying at an early age. "I used to hang around Morrison's Flying Service in Helena and bum rides with anyone who would take me up," he recalled. Later, while attending the University of Montana in Missoula, he became a smokejumper and "got to

54

GARRY WUNDERWALD

JOHN REDDY

NEAL & MARY JANE MISHLER

Left: *Montana is a headwaters state.*
Above: *Spring run-off turns a river like the Middle Fork of the Flathead into a white-knuckle, whitewater thrill.*
Top: *Morning comes to Glacier National Park.*

know the pilots over there." At the time, he was temporarily sidetracked by a major in marketing and advertising at the university.

"One quarter away from graduating, I realized I didn't want to move to New Jersey or Philadelphia to work in advertising," he said. "I wanted to stay in Montana to hunt and fish and fly airplanes." Within six months, after completing a federally sponsored aviation course, he was hired as a co-pilot for Western Airlines. After a year with Western, he moved over to TWA, where he's been ever since.

Spending two thirds of every month away from home has heightened Ashcraft's appreciation of his native state. "For so long, I took Montana for granted," he said. "Now I realize that people spend thousands of dollars to come out here for a once-in-a-lifetime hunting trip."

Through the usual on-the-job chatter about home and family, Ashcraft has come to appreciate other Montana values. "My colleagues are surprised to learn that I still get together with the guys I went to school with," he said. "I think we are uniquely interested in the people we grew up with. It's not that we care how much money they're making, but how they're doing, whether they're happy."

MICHAEL CRUMMETT

TWA pilot Larry Ashcraft is one of an estimated 50 commercial pilots who live in Montana and commute to work all over the globe.

Browning High School Principal J.R. Clark has a problem. He can hardly get a toot out of the Browning High band, which has diminished from 160 students to 30 in just six years. During the same period, the choral department has swelled from seven to 170.

Ever since a former Arizona nightclub performer named Barbara Chase showed up at Browning High in 1982, chorus is cool. "It's been very damaging to our band program," said Clark, only half-disappointed. If that were the extent of his problems, he would be a happy man. "We have two state champion wrestlers, plus the majority of the boys' basketball team in chorus," he said. "We have kids with four-point averages and kids ready to be kicked out of school. The only thing that's keeping them in is chorus."

"She's the light in our forest," said Clark of the popular teacher who came to Montana one summer to perform for Glacier Park tourists and wound up on the Blackfeet Indian Reservation, turning kids on to music and on to themselves.

To see the Browning High men's ensemble or senior girls' choir perform at the State Music Festival is to understand music as therapy. One of the boys has a black eye; one of the girls is pregnant. For many of them, survival is a challenge, and life can be as harsh as the winter winds that sweep down on Browning from the Rocky Mountain Front. But when they're on stage, these kids are all hugs and smiles. While other groups strive for perfect pitch, the Browning High singers specialize in spirit.

"Enthusiasm is our thing," said Chase. "I know I teach music well, but in Browning, I also teach self-pride and self-worth. I teach goals because these kids don't have many."

Chase is quick to point out that her relationship with her students is not a one-way deal: "I've learned as much as they have." She has quit wondering how she ever got to Browning in the first place; now, she wonders whether she'll be able to leave. A talented performer who has never stayed in one place very long, she misses the stage and the travel that goes with it. "Every year, I say this is my last, I've got to get out of here," she said. "But these kids keep me here. They love me and they know I love them. They deserve a chance."

MICHAEL CRUMMETT PHOTOS

Above: *Browning High chorus teacher Barbara Chase teaches spirit and self-pride on the Blackfeet Indian Reservation.* **Below:** *Suzanna McDougal raises flowers for the "ever-lasting" market and more than a hundred varieties of herbs on her acre outside Hamilton.*

Farming and ranching constitute one of Montana's most exclusive societies. Unless you're born to it or marry into it, agriculture is off limits to all but the wealthiest or most resourceful people. Suzanna McDougal is one of the latter.

With one acre under intensive cultivation behind her house on the outskirts of Hamilton, McDougal is on her way to achieving a lifetime goal. *"One Acre and Security.* That's the name of a book my mother gave a long time ago," said McDougal. "That's what I'm working on."

On her acre, McDougal raises flowers and more than a hundred varieties of herbs for her business, Mountain Butterfly Herbs. The flowers are dried for the "everlasting" market. Bunches of dried baby's breath, statice and lunaria hang from the rafters of her garage. Soon they will be part of a wreath or a floral arrangement or a gift of potpourri. Outside in the garden are row after row of French tarragon, lovage, skullcap and dozens of other exotic and common herbs raised for the culinary and medicinal markets. Beside the garden is an old egg incubator, where McDougal is drying a batch of shepherd's purse, which will be sold to midwives to soothe and calm their patients.

A range of customers, including florists, area restaurants, natural food stores and manufacturers of herbal extracts, keep her busy year-round. From May through October, she is busy harvesting and distributing her produce. During the winter, she cultivates the business, developing new markets, improving her packaging and conducting workshops.

"Farming is amazing work," she said. "There are so many different aspects to it. One day I'm a carpenter, the next day I'm marketing or working on propagation, composting or soil preparation."

McDougal, who was raised on a dairy farm in Michigan and moved to Montana in the mid-1970s, said anyone can get into the business: "Once you've got the land, the overhead is minimal. All you need is a truck, a greenhouse, a rototiller and a shredder-grinder."

Strolling down the rows of her garden, she and her visitor grazed on fresh sorrel and licorice mint. Moving over to a patch of lavendar, she described the aromatic herb as a soothing addition to bathwater. "Just smelling the leaf is wonderful, isn't it?"

Right: *Windsurfing on Lower St. Mary's Lake, Glacier National Park.*
Below: *The Bitterroot Valley is dotted with small farms.*
Bottom: *Clark Canyon Reservoir and nearby Lima Peaks at sunset.*

MICHAEL CRUMMETT

TOM DIETRICH

TOM DIETRICH

The nation's best supply of standing, dead lodgepole pine brought Ken Thuerbach to Montana 16 years ago. He was 26 at the time, a recent graduate of the Harvard Business School, and anxious to test a new idea he had about on-site construction of log homes. He had read somewhere that by 1990, there would no longer be craftsmen in America who could build authentic log homes. Today, he is the world's largest manufacturer of authentic log homes.

MICHAEL CRUMMETT

Entrepreneur Ken Thuerbach pioneered the log home business in the Bitterroot Valley.

Facing page: *Cottonwoods catch the last light of an autumn day on the Little Blackfoot River.*

When Thuerbach moved Alpine Log Homes from Colorado to Victor, he was the only log-home builder in the Bitterroot Valley. Today, there are 23. With the proliferation of these companies in Western Montana, you might think that if you've seen one log home, you've seen them all. Chances are, you have not seen an Alpine home and probably will not, because 99 percent are shipped out of state, log by log, on flatbed trucks.

Alpine specializes in quality. Workers in the pre-assembly log yard at Victor are described by Thuerbach as artisans and craftsmen. Bark is peeled by hand. Logs are hand-notched. Customers with names like Perot and Naisbitt fly their own aircraft into Victor for consultation sessions with the designers at Alpine. In addition to one-of-a-kind, luxury homes for an upscale, residential market, Alpine builds corporate retreats, lodges, condominiums, churches and museums, and ships them coast to coast.

The cost of shipping logs across the country is offset by the centralization of materials, equipment, architects and designers at Victor. Thuerbach gets the credit for pioneering this concept in the industry. He has also designed many of the tools that are used industry-wide—like electric chisels and something he describes as a "tractor with an ice tong." Thuerbach takes pride in running a clean operation and contributing to the economic well-being of the Bitterroot Valley. "We have never cut live trees," he said. "We give the bark to area ranchers for bedding, and much of the scrap goes to the elderly for firewood. There is no burning, no smoke, no chemicals."

He is one of those "new" Montanans who brought to the state not only a business but also a vision of what a business can be. He regards Montana as having lots of potential for innovators and works with other businesspeople in the area to nurture their ideas. "The more successful people we have in Montana, the better off we'll be," he said.

Most farmers just shake their heads when they hear about Bob Quinn's organic wheat milling and shipping operation in Fort Benton. When they learn they cannot use any chemicals if they want to market their wheat through his Montana Wheat and Flour, Inc., you can almost hear them say to themselves, "But we've never done it that way." Still, they're curious. In an era of unpredictable prices for Montana's largest grain crop, the organic market not only pays well; it's growing.

PAT O'HARA

Quinn discovered the market when he was in California, studying for a master's degree in plant biochemistry. Organically grown, high-protein wheat was in demand by large whole-grain bakeries that were supplying the health-conscious market of southern California. Disenchanted with the California lifestyle, Quinn returned to his native Big Sandy after earning his degree, and took over the family farm. It was not long before he was also sending truckloads of stone-ground, organic wheat to California. His market now includes bakeries in Utah and New Jersey, as well as a few steady customers in Montana.

"There's still lots of skepticism among Montana farmers about growing wheat organically," Quinn said. "But I think we need to look for every possible niche to add value to our product."

When he first opened the milling business, he saw his product simply as a commercial response to a market demand. On his own farm, he kept growing wheat the way it had always been grown, with plenty of assistance from fertilizers and pesticides. Through the business, however, he learned about medical problems associated with chemically treated grains and decided to "grow organic" himself. He is now a believer.

"It's appealing to me to have a renewable resource that's sustainable without chemical inputs," he said. "Chemicals and fertilizers are expensive, and they may not always be available."

Judging from the small but steady growth of his business, it appears that others are reaching the same conclusion.

Bob Quinn markets organic wheat to whole-grain bakeries in California, Utah, New Jersey and Montana.

As a professional assignment, Montana is widely regarded as a plum among resource managers. What is not so well known is that Montana also ranks high as a permanent home for retired resource professionals. Within the past 10 years, the retired directors of three of the top federal resource agencies in the state have made Montana their personal as well as their professional choice.

All three—Tom Coston, Ed "Moose" Zaidlicz and Bob Haraden—were raised outside Montana and had plenty of opportunities to compare states as they rose through the ranks of the U.S. Forest Service (USFS), the Bureau of Land Management (BLM) and the National Park Service (NPS) respectively. Together, they have probably lived and worked in 25 states, from Maine to California, Mississippi to Alaska. Yet, it was the Rocky Mountain states, and particularly Montana, that felt like home when it came time to sink roots.

Melvin Lammi operates one of the few ferries on the Missouri River, at Carter.

TIM CHRISTIE

"I used the same yardstick for every state," said former Montana BLM Director Zaidlicz, who has lived in Billings since 1969. "But they just didn't measure up to Montana."

The obvious attraction was the environment and all it has to offer three men who made their careers managing public lands. "You're nuts if you don't take advantage of it," Zaidlicz said one December day as he finished off a batch of hand-tied flies he calls "cream scud" in preparation for a fishing trip on the Yellowstone.

But just as important as place to these men and their families are the people and the lifestyle of Montana. Honest, direct, friendly and tolerant are some of the adjectives they use to describe the people they have come to know as their neighbors.

Coston, who served as chief of the USFS Northern Region in Missoula from 1979 to 1986, said he relished the controversy that went with the job not so much because of the issues but because of the attitudes of the people involved. "People here are very forgiving," he said. "After hammering away at one another one day, you can sit down with them over a cup of coffee the next day and talk about hunting. You can be an avid environmentalist and still get along with your neighbor, even though he works in a sawmill."

Below: A golden sunset in Montana's Golden Valley County.
Right: *Familiar sight in Montana's back country.*

MICHAEL CRUMMETT

Retired forester Tom Coston said he knew he was home when he first came to Montana as a kid from Tennessee.

MICHAEL CRUMMETT PHOTOS

Retired BLM Director Ed "Moose" Zaidlicz said he used the same yardstick for every state, "but they just didn't measure up to Montana."

Both Coston and Zaidlicz set their sights on Montana early on. "When I first came to Montana as a kid from Tennessee, I knew I was home," said Coston.

For Zaidlicz, it took a little longer. After serving as a navigator-bombardier in World War II, the Pittsburgh native came to Montana for a week of hunting with an Air Force buddy from Billings. "When I stepped off the plane, I thought the Yellowstone Valley was the most beautiful place I'd ever seen," he recalled. It took him more than 20 years to get back to Montana, but he never lost sight of the goal.

Zaidlicz is just plain in love with the state—its people, its resources, its history, even its weather. The son of Polish immigrants, he likes to tell stories and one of his favorites is about a trip he took to North Dakota several years ago as Montana BLM director. "It was a frigid day in Bismarck, and I was giving the governor a bad time about the weather in North Dakota," he recalled. "The governor just smiled and pulled a button out from under his coat that said, 'Minus 44 degrees keeps the riffraff out'."

Whatever it is that holds a lid on the population in these parts, Zaidlicz is for it. "The fact that you can still get away for two or three days and not see a soul is a privilege you can't disregard," he said. "And when you do run into someone in the woods, you never know whether it will be a trapper or a college professor. In some cases, it's both."

One of Zaidlicz's favorite retreats is the Missouri River below Fort Benton. During his tenure as state BLM director, he implemented its designation as a U.S. Wild and Scenic River—protective status that had been won by U.S. Senator Lee Metcalf.

Born and raised on the coast of Maine, former Glacier National Park Superintendent Bob Haraden had a gut feeling he needed water in his life, so he and his wife "poked around the Pacific Northwest" when it came time to think about retirement. But it was too late; Montana had a firm grip on the Haradens. They settled in Bozeman after leaving Glacier in 1986 and solved the water problem by acquiring a summer cabin on Seeley Lake.

Haraden believes he is the only NPS professional to have worked in all of the "Big Four" of the Rocky Mountain region—Rocky Mountain, Grand Teton, Yellowstone and Glacier national parks. "While we have been privileged to live in some of America's greatest parks," he said, "there is none as spectacular as Glacier, either in the United States or the Alps of Europe."

MICHAEL K. FRANCIS

JOHN REDDY

GARRY WUNDERWALD

Above: *Quiet afternoon on Holland Lake.*
Left: *Bighorn sheep are among Montana's treasured wildlife resources.*
Top: *Summer is short in the high country of the Absaroka-Beartooth Wilderness.*

Haraden grabbed the opportunity to work as superintendent of Glacier in 1981 because of the "kind and complexity" of the resource issues he would be handling. "Glacier is a place where you can make some headway on issues," he explained. "The problems are solvable," he added, but said he worries about encroachment "on all sides" of Glacier, ranging from oil exploration and coal development to helicopter flights and acid rain.

Both natives of New England, Bob and Adelaide Haraden are right at home in Montana. "We have developed a real kinship with the people of Montana who made us feel welcome and at home the day we arrived," Bob said.

MICHAEL CRUMMETT

Above: *Former Glacier National Park Superintendent Bob Haraden grew up in Maine but regards Montana as home.*
Facing page: *Just knowing that places like the Spanish Lakes in the Lee Metcalf Wilderness exist is a comfort to residents and visitors alike.*

Even though all three men have stepped down from their professional positions of leadership, they continue to give generous portions of their time and wisdom to their adopted state. In Missoula, Coston helped organize a new, non-profit organization called the Bob Marshall Foundation to raise donated funds for trail restoration in the Bob Marshall wildlands complex. In Bozeman, Haraden volunteers his time to his former agency, conducting oral history interviews with some of the "old-timers in the park service" and inspecting national historic landmarks administered by the NPS in Montana. And in Billings, Zaidlicz divides his time between local service projects for underprivileged, abused and neglected kids and advisory work for state agencies. He is a former member of the Montana Board of Health and Environmental Sciences and served as chairman of the Governor's Council on Montanans Outdoors in 1986.

Provincial as natives can be on the subject of "outsiders," none can deny the contributions made by the many non-natives who have made Montana their home. These three men—Coston, Zaidlicz and Haraden—have set a high standard for natives and newcomers alike.

PAT O'HARA

3
THE MONTANA GRIP:
IT WON'T LET GO

On any given day, a Montanan can point to at least one good reason to pull up stakes. For rural residents, it gets old having to drive a hundred miles, one way, to see the dentist, buy a new Maytag or catch a movie. Even the majority of Montanans who are classified as urban are subject to merchants who will be happy to order the shower door or spare part they need right now. Beyond the sheer inconvenience of living in what has come to be known as the "empty quarter" of North America, there is the persistent threat of the weather or the economy pulling the rug out from under us.

MICHAEL CRUMMETT

Montanans are accustomed to traveling long distances on lonely highways.

Facing page: *Montana's outdoor recreation and its world-class hunting and fishing have a firm grip on most Montanans.*

But just when we think we have had it with Montana—the love affair is over—the cattle market turns around, we get two inches of rain, or we have our best fishing season ever. Try as we may, we can't leave. Somewhere along the line, when we weren't looking, the love affair grew into a commitment. And, like any worthwhile relationship, this one has its ups and downs.

A Missoula woman in her 70s is back home from California, where she lived for several years. She enjoys weekly hiking and skiing outings with her friends but said "you have to be a psychic masochist to put up with Montana's inconvenience and politics."

A Helena couple has tried to leave the state twice in the past five years. Both attorneys, they had good jobs lined up on the East Coast. Last time they left, they got the furniture all the way to Virginia before they turned around. Just like the first time, it was the fly fishing and friends that brought them back home.

Montana's outdoor recreation, its world-class hunting and fishing, have a firm grip on most Montanans. A five-minute drive to work, and no standing in line for chairlifts or postal clerks are equally compelling attractions. Newcomers delight in the Montana lifestyle; natives are simply spoiled by it.

But there are more fundamental attractions that bind us to our Montana home. Like people the world over, we are drawn to the familiar, and nothing is more familiar than the family and the community in which we grew up.

GARRY WUNDERWALD

There is comfort here, a way of life that worked for the folks, so why not for us? There are neighbors and old friends we can count on. In the case of many Montanans, there is a piece of land that's been under the stewardship of one family for three or four generations. Attachment to the land is a sacred matter for Montana's Indian tribes. Generations of Blackfeet and Crow Indians have sought visions, communed with the Thunderbird and worshipped the Creator in sanctuaries that we know as Chief Mountain, the Sweetgrass Hills and the Crazies.

These are the bonds that will not let us give up on Montana.

Butte loyalists Margie McGowan, Mary Ellen Cromrich and Ellen Warner have commuted to work in Helena five days a week for the past six years.

MICHAEL CRUMMETT

Mark Sullivan, *district judge, Butte:*

"We had our last child while we were living in Helena but I took my wife to Butte for the delivery so our boy would have a Butte birthright."

Five days a week for the past six years, Ellen Warner, Margie McGowan and Mary Ellen Cromrich have put in 12-hour days for their employer, US WEST Communications, formerly Mountain Bell. They spend eight hours on the job in Helena and up to four hours on the road. It is the price of keeping a residence in Butte, and for these Butte natives, it is worth it.

"I enjoy Helena, but Butte is my home," said Mary Ellen, a service representative for the telephone company for the past 15 years. Twice since 1982, when Mountain Bell closed its Butte office, Cromrich has moved to Helena. She lasted two years away from Butte the first time, the second time only a year and a half.

"You just can't get away from Butte," she said.

Ellen and Margie do not even try. "We all have our families, our homes and our heritage in Butte," said Ellen, who has worked for the company for 25 years. Margie has been with the company for 10 years. All three were unwilling to abandon good jobs with the company when Mountain Bell abandoned Butte.

So every morning about 6:30, they head north to Helena. By the time they are home again, it is 6:30 p.m. It has not been easy. The life of a commuter is a trade-off at best. They have missed countless kids' school programs and other activities. But by the time they get home, cranky customers and other job-related problems are forgotten; they can give their full attention to their families.

In six years, they have missed only one day of work due to bad weather. During that time, they have missed work on March 17 six times. "We always take St. Patrick's Day off," said Margie. "We sign up well in advance to make **S**sure we get it off."

Sandra Cahill routinely receives love letters from all over the world. Her admirers range in age from 4 to 80. Their occupations and lifestyles are as varied as their ages, but when they are with Sandra, they are equal, especially when she puts them on top of a horse for the first time.

As head wrangler at the 63 Ranch south of Livingston, Sandra guides her

Right: *Nearly one third of all Montanans hunt big game or upland birds.*
Below: *Remnants of a Blackfeet Sun Dance lodge in the Two Medicine River country.*

GARRY WUNDERWALD

MICHAEL CRUMMETT

MICHAEL CRUMMETT

MICHAEL CRUMMETT

CHARLES KAY

Above: *Accessible, watchable wildlife is an important part of the Montana lifestyle.*
Left: *A popular event on the Fort Belknap Indian Reservation is the annual "Mosquito Run."*
Top: *Montana's homestead era is evident on farms and fields across the state.*

The 63 Ranch, south of Livingston, has been capturing the hearts of "dudes" since 1929. Jinnie Christensen and her daughter, Sandra Cahill, own and manage the guest ranch.

MICHAEL CRUMMETT

Chuck Murphy, *rancher, Musselshell, on the subject of his neighbors, known as the "Bull Mountain Savages":*

"We've worked together so long, we know what needs to be done without being told. If something happens to one of our families, our neighbors know our business better than we do and the work just goes on."

world-traveled guests into places of the heart, places like Agate Springs and Silver Pass, Hellroaring Divide and Rainbow Lakes Plateau.

"I feel very connected to you and to this land," a New York doctor told her after one week at the 63. "It's important to know that this land is here and that it doesn't change."

The kids are less philosophical. One, who signed his name, "Jonny," wrote: "I like it better At the Dude Ranch then At my house. You were my Best friend when we were there. Is Sparkle O.K.?"

The 63 has been capturing the hearts of visitors since 1929, when Sandra's father, Paul Christensen, and his brother and sister bought the land from original homesteaders. "Their dream was to find the perfect location and build a dude ranch," said Sandra. "And that's what they did." Four years later, Paul married Virginia Bevin, a dude from New York City who embraced the western lifestyle. She soon became "Jinnie" and a full partner in the business.

Just south of Livingston, at the north end of the Absaroka Range, the 63 presents its visitors with sweeping views of the Crazies, the Bridgers and the Castle Mountains to the north and northwest. To the south and southeast are Yellowstone Park and the Absaroka-Beartooth Wilderness. So vast is the neighborhood that Sandra seldom takes the same ride twice as she guides some 200 guests each summer.

Beginning in June, guests start arriving for one- and two-week vacations; many come year after year. Like the doctor from New York, they seem to need assurance that some things do not change. "I tried to soak up enough forests, mountains, meadows, creeks, horses and friendly people to last till next year," wrote one guest, "but I know it definitely takes longer than a week."

According to Sandra, it's the lure of the West and the personal touch at the 63 that keeps them coming back from France, Germany, New York and California. "We try to extend to our guests what we would to any guest visiting a home in Montana," she said. "We ride with them, we eat with them, and we do a lot of extra things for them."

Sandra and her family lean on the horses to do the rest: "Some people re-enact the dream of a lifetime by coming out here and getting on a horse."

From time to time, Jim Curtis, D.V.M., suspects his life on the high plains of Northeastern Montana is merely a fantasy. It's too good to be true. Living in the midst of historic cattle and sheep ranches, a charter member of the annual Milk River Wagon Train, a collector and fixer of antique wagons and other prairie "junk," a horse trader and storyteller at heart, Dr. Curtis datelines his correspondence: "Malta, center of the universe." A native of Great Falls, he has become a thoroughgoing "Hi-Liner" and a keen observer of the Eastern Montana mindset.

72

Malta veterinarian Jim Curtis views Montana as a natural filter for the kind of people he likes to live with.

Tat Cain, businessman, Miles City:

"We're the friendly people. None of us is gonna make enough money to leave town, so we have to get along."

He views Montana as a natural filter for the kind of people he likes to live with because "Montana—especially, Eastern Montana—won't support artificial life.

"Eastern Montanans are incredibly resilient creatures," he adds. "They're like coyotes."

Curtis, president of the Montana Veterinary Association, warns would-be veterinarians that they won't get rich in Montana but "they will have fun and they will be able to tell their kids what they do for a living." He has great affection for his clientele and worries visibly about their welfare. After performing one of the first caesarean sections of the 1988 calving season, he explained the economics of the procedure: "This heifer is worth $700 and its calf should be worth $400. From that, deduct an hour of the rancher's time trying to deliver the calf himself, an hour driving the cow to Malta, an hour of my time, an hour driving the cow and new calf back home and another hour mothering up the calf when he gets home. The heifer probably can't be bred again, and the rancher doesn't know what the calf will be worth a year from now, or even whether the calf will live."

"The whole thing is a gamble," he added. "But everyone knows ranching is more than a living. It's a lifestyle, and I'm in the same trap. But what the hell else would I rather do? This is fun."

Just a few miles off Interstate 90, south of Manhattan, lies an invisible community of 2,000 Dutch farmers and ranchers. Topping the rise that leads into Churchill, you would never know you were in the midst of one of Montana's most cohesive ethnic communities. There are a few giveaways—mailboxes with names like Feddes and Flikkema, an occasional windmill or a highway sign announcing Amsterdam or Wooden Shoe Road. Otherwise, Churchill is just another sleepy town on another quiet backroad. Hardly a town at all, Churchill has no bars, no stores, no restaurants or cafes.

What Churchill does have, as its name implies, is a church. Not one but two. Not Lutheran and Catholic but Calvinist and Calvinist. Not morning or evening services but morning *and* evening services. On Sunday, Churchill is one busy place. New Pontiacs and Buicks overflow the parking lots of the First Christian Reformed Church and the Bethel Christian Reformed Church, less than two city blocks apart. From all corners of the Gallatin valley, the Lord's handsome, blond flock has arrived.

"You don't see the communities of Churchill and Amsterdam until Sunday because they're scattered over the golden hills of the Gallatin Valley," according to Dr. Rob Kroes, a former visiting professor at Montana State University (MSU) from the University of Amsterdam in the Netherlands. "Both literally and metaphorically, they come together at church."

One member of the community, Mary Swier-Bolhuis, described the relationship between church and Churchill-Amsterdam this way: "Church is what our community is all about. We arrange our lives around it. Everyone attends every wedding and every funeral. Sunday services are held in the

Right: *The Milk River Wagon Train is a favorite event of Montana's Hi-Liners.*
Below: *Gallatin County's Dutch community comes together every Sunday at church.*

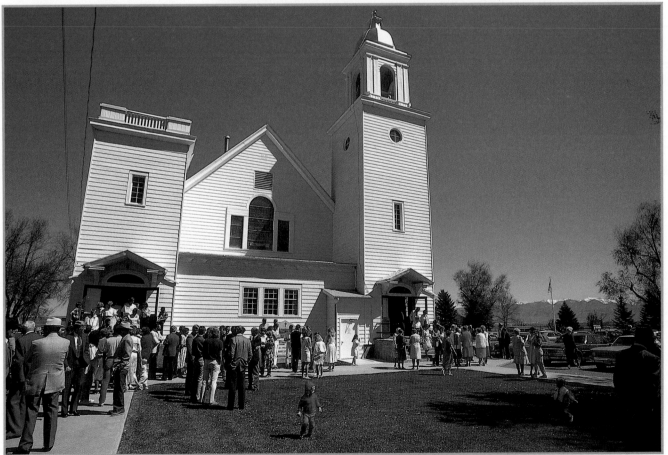

MICHAEL CRUMMETT PHOTOS BOTH PAGES

morning and evening, and that's not for the sake of convenience. You don't go to either service; you go to both."

Swier-Bolhuis said she "can't imagine anyone *not* attending church," a hunch that is confirmed by church membership. Until 1960, there was just one Christian Reformed Church in the community. Overflow crowds necessitated construction of the Bethel church, and now, nearly 1,200 people attend one or the other. Another 500 Dutch from the valley attend Christian Reformed Church services in Bozeman and Gallatin Gateway.

Come Monday, the male residents of Churchill and Amsterdam are back at work on their highly productive farms, raising seed potatoes, grain and hay or tending their dairy herds. The women are, for the most part, in their homes, tending large families.

A degree in ag economics from MSU or attendance at one of the church's three affiliated liberal arts colleges in the nation helps assure that Dutch will marry Dutch and come home to "the church on the hill."

If you have attended an Indian basketball game or tried to find a seat in a hospital waiting room when an Indian is hospitalized, you have had a glimpse of Indian family life. To understand the importance of family relations among Indians, it is helpful to understand the relative unimportance of nearly everything else.

Janine Pease Windy Boy is the founding president of the Little Bighorn College on the Crow Reservation. She has also served as president of the American Indian Higher Education Consortium, an organization of tribal

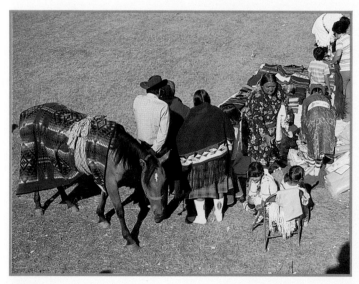

Below: *Crow family giving away blankets, shawls and a Pendleton-wrapped horse.* **Facing page:** *Crow Fair dancer.*

colleges throughout the United States. Impressive credentials in the eyes of a white achiever. But they mean little to either Janine or her fellow members of the Crow Tribe.

"Who I am and who I'm related to are more important to my people than what I do," she said. "The hierarchy of our tribe is based on a lifetime of living, not on the job you hold or the money you make."

To understand the depth and complexity of relationships in the Crow Tribe, you would have to enroll in the three-hour course on kinship at Little Bighorn College. There, you would learn about the Crow clan system, which unites several families matrilineally, or through the mother. No matter how remote the blood lines are within a clan, clan members feel a close sense of kinship and rely on one another for support and protection.

There are at least 50 different terms for blood relations and these, Janine explained, involve more than the genetic bond: "The ethic of how you treat one another is important to this network of relationships." For example, a man will always put his sister's husband above himself as an expression of love for his sister. To avoid spats and quarreling, a husband never speaks to his mother-in-law or sister-in-law. This avoidance measure also prevents the relationship from straying into forbidden territory.

Crows honor their family and clan relations by heaping gifts on them.

The traditional Crow "giveaway" celebrates significant occasions like a birthday or graduation, the naming of a child or a basketball championship. Typical gifts are horses, rifles, blankets, shawls, yardage and shirts, and gifts go to "the prominent people in your life," according to Janine, "the name-givers, the people who call on you in time of illness or misfortune."

A lifetime of support from family and clan relations makes it difficult for a Crow to leave the reservation. Of 8,000 enrolled members of the tribe, 5,000 live on the reservation. "It's hard to be away from here," said Janine, who knows because she has tried.

"I am strong because I am empowered by my clan relatives," she said. "How can I be strong without that support?"

Driving over the frozen tundra of Northeastern Montana on a sub-zero February day, it is hard to imagine ever being warm again. Snow squeals on contact with hard rubber; descending temperatures transform imperceptible moisture into ice crystals against a brilliant blue sky. Reaching the turnoff for the Turner Hutterite colony—25 miles north of Harlem, 12 miles south of the Canadian border—you glance back as a ground blizzard erases Highway 241, shift into four-wheel drive and hope you will be able to find your way back to civilization before dark.

Preacher John and wife Annie Hofer of the Turner Hutterite Colony.

Soon, you are surrounded by half a dozen charming, chattering women, who rush you into a kitchen that feels, at once, like home. After three hours of good talk, laughter and oceans of coffee, you wish you could stay for a week.

The womenfolk of the Turner Colony are as curious about you as you are about them. Trading questions about jobs and roles, husbands and kids, they are eager to explain a lifestyle that is grounded in four centuries of religious tradition.

Hutterite colonies are organized as work and family units. Generally, one man, who is designated as the preacher, plus his brothers and their families, make up a colony; when one colony outgrows the basic farm-ranch operation, it is time to split off and start production on a new piece of land. The Turner Colony, established in 1957, is a spinoff of a colony near Grassrange that outgrew itself.

At the heart of every colony is a philosophy of communal sharing and caring. "There are no orphans or widows here," said Annie Hofer, wife of preacher John Hofer, the "head guy" at Turner Colony. "We work for the colony and the colony takes care of us."

Hutterite men work the land and raise the livestock. Women handle all the sewing, cooking and baking. Children are educated through the 10th grade; at age 17, they begin a lifetime of work for the colony. Between the ages of 18 and 24, when they are "old enough to know right from wrong," young people are baptized. Only then are they ready for marriage. Hutterite girls are required to marry outside the colony. When they marry, they take up residence in their husband's colony. There are no divorces among Hutterites. If there is an unhappy marriage, it is "fixed" by the preacher.

What some would reject as a stifling, drab existence is embraced as a life of fulfillment and joy by Judy Hofer, John and Annie's daughter. In her early

Top: *Blaine County's Turner Hutterite Colony, 12 miles south of the Canadian border.*
Above: *John and Annie's daughter, Judy Hofer, loves to sew and sing and play her guitar.*
Right: *Elizabeth Hofer gives the morning ration of milk to freshly-weaned calves.*

MICHAEL CRUMMETT PHOTOS BOTH PAGES

Clockwise from top left:
Frank Stahl pours a round of toasts as new wife Kathy holds the tray.
Betty Marie Hofer.
Jerry Hofer with red fox catch.
Judy Hofer sings country western at her sister's wedding chivaree.

20s, Judy is radiantly alive and very much at peace with her world. She has yet to be baptized or married, and she is in no hurry. She wants to be sure. In the meantime, she enjoys the adornment of a ring and earrings that will "come off forever" when she is baptized. She delights in playing the "straight man" to her cousin in a line of jokes about Hutterites obviously aimed to put visitors at ease. An accomplished seamstress, she takes pride in the western-cut jackets she has sewn for herself and her siblings. Like everyone in her family, she loves parties and looks forward to the annual Milk River Wagon Train, when residents of Blaine and Phillips counties get together for a campfire cookout on the last night of the event. "I just love the cowboys," she beamed.

While not rushing toward marriage, Judy likes to think about the prospect and looks forward to the marathon celebration that cements every Hutterite marriage. The ritual gets underway on Monday with picnics, parties, prayer meetings and chivarees. On Sunday, the bride and groom are married in the presence of 400-500 friends and relatives from other colonies. By Sunday night, everyone understands that this marriage is intended to last.

While Judy is prepared to leave the colony when the time comes for her to marry, she could never leave the Hutterite way of life. "I love my parents too much," she said. Mother Annie is more succinct: "You'd be lost."

Montana's Hutterites are flourishing. An estimated 50 colonies, averaging about 75 members each, have grown from Montana's first colony, established near Lewistown in 1936. The explanation may be found in Annie Hofer's simple philosophy: "Live and let live."

Harlem and Helena may exist within the borders of the same state but that is about all they have common. Helena's day-to-day preoccupation with politics, bureaucracy and budgets has little relevance to the farmers and livestock producers of Blaine County.

"People up here are more interested in trying to make a living," said one Blaine County native who is at home in both worlds. Since 1958, Francis Bardanouve has divided his time between biennial, January through April, sessions of the Montana Legislature and his combined farm and ranch operation outside of Harlem. He is the current dean of the Legislature, having served 15 terms in the House of Representatives, eight of those as chairman of the all-important House Appropriations Committee.

"I'll be away all winter, and the folks around here hardly know I'm gone," said Bardanouve, who is rarely opposed in his legislative campaigns. "Occasionally, I'll run into someone in town who asks me how things are going in Washington."

Bardanouve is a rancher first, raising cattle on land that was settled by his grandparents before World War I. He has diversified and expanded the original home ranch to include a wheat farm and a second ranch south of Chinook. But a visit to his home reveals that his career as a legislator runs a close second. Thick, government documents and a stack of mail are piled up on the floor beside his favorite chair, ready for his attention when he gets in from feeding his livestock. The phone is within reach of the same chair. One wall of his basement office is lined with periodicals that keep him current with the world beyond Harlem. The rest of the office is filled with memorabilia from 30 years in public

Janice Downey, Butte native living in Missoula:
"I don't feel compelled to live there but I don't want to get too far away. I never want to be more than two hours from Butte."

Harlem and Helena are worlds apart but veteran legislator Francis Bardanouve is at home in both.

office—snapshots and autographed photos of U.S. Sen. Mike Mansfield, Gov. Ted Schwinden and other friends in Democratic politics; a fencepost signed by the members of the legislature; a pair of work boots, polished up and painted gold, presented to him by a group of legislative employees after his unsuccessful attempt to abolish the Governor's Inaugural Ball as a waste of taxpayers' money.

In Helena, Bardanouve is the taxpayer's best friend. He has a reputation of being "tight with the dollar," as he put it. He also has a reputation for hard work and dedication. "He knows the state's business better than anyone else," said Venus, his wife of 20 years. Few would disagree.

"If I had to choose between the ranch and legislature, it would be a tough choice because I like them both, but probably the legislature would have to go," he said. "When I'm in Helena and I hear on the radio that it's 35 below on the Hi-Line, I don't miss the ranch a bit. But when it starts warming up, I sure want to be back here, calving and seeding."

With little more than a well-worn pair of shoes, a guitar, a camera and a notebook, Walkin' Jim Stoltz is the free spirit we all long to be. As his name implies, Walkin' Jim prefers to see the country by foot. He's logged more than 16,000 miles, trekking from Mexico to Canada and from the Atlantic to the Pacific, but when it's time to give his feet a rest, Walkin' Jim comes home to Montana.

"I wasn't really looking for a place to live when I came through Montana on my coast to coast walk in 1976," he said, "but when I got here, I loved all the wild country and the songs that came from Montana."

Ironically, it's that combination of wild country and songs that take Walkin' Jim away from Montana every year. During the fall, he takes his ballads from the back country on tour, performing for outdoor clubs and community concerts, elementary schools and universities across the country.

Arnold Bolle, retired Dean of the UM Forestry School, Missoula:
"Because of Montana's sparse population, people know one another across the state. After four or five meetings, you know everyone who's involved in the issues you're involved in."

Walkin' Jim Stoltz loves the "wild country and the songs that come from Montana."

BERT LINDLER

You tramp across the ridgeline as the world spreads down below,
And you're feelin' like a king just a-hoardin' o'er his gold,
You think that if you take another breath you'll just explode
And you feel the choir a-singin' in your soul.

He's been described by critics across the nation as "part of the soul of America" and "a folk singer in the grand tradition set by Woody Guthrie," but Montana audiences are just getting acquainted with Walkin' Jim as the troubadour who led a two-month Bob Marshall Trek around the perimeter of the wilderness area in 1987. Organized by the Montana Wilderness Association to draw attention to problems of encroachment facing the Bob Marshall ecosystem, the Trek offered Walkin' Jim the opportunity to "do something" to try to protect the wild country he loves. "It took me about five minutes to decide to do it," he recalled. Highlights of the trip included a Fourth of July celebration on

Above: *During the 1987 Bob Marshall Trek, hikers celebrated Marshall's birthday with cake and balloons.*
Right: *Walkin' Jim prefers to view the world from the top*

Rocky Mountain Peak and a birthday party, complete with cake and balloons, for Bob Marshall.

The images and music that grew out of the Trek trace a journey that all Montanans can enjoy, regardless of whether they will ever set foot on a hiking trail. Montanans take pleasure in just knowing that land is out there, and Walkin' Jim is the guy who reminds us it's still there, as rugged and vulnerable as ever.

The road to Leah Cole's place, 40 miles northeast of Jordan, passes through three distinct ecosystems: first, a bright red, sun-baked desert; then, the lunar landscape of the Missouri River Breaks and badlands; finally, the surprise of cool pines and cottonwoods that line the fingers of Fort Peck Lake.

Third-generation Garfield County rancher Leah Cole.

On a good day, the drive takes a little over an hour. On anything less than a dry day, call first. Asked what is the longest period she ever has been weathered in, Leah responded matter-of-factly: "Seven months."

"I kind of enjoy getting snowed in," she said. "It forces you to relax."

Leah Cole's idea of a vacation is staying home and taking the phone off the hook for two weeks. A livestock order buyer, she spends hours every day on the phone during shipping season, connecting Central and Eastern Montana livestock producers with Midwestern feedlots. When she's not on the phone, she travels a huge triangle, roughly bordered by Lewistown, Circle and Malta, to keep current with area livestock producers and their market needs.

That is her off-farm job. Leah Cole has done "just about everything" to stay on the land her grandfather "proved up" in 1913. She has operated a commercial fishery on Fort Peck Lake, outfitted hunters and trapped coyotes. And along with her neighbors, she has fought to maintain grazing rights on the C.M. Russell National Wildlife Refuge that surrounds her land.

"Between paying off loans, raising kids, fighting muddy roads and trying to save our grazing rights, I've fought hard to stay on this land," she said. "It's no wonder I want to stay right here."

"Right here" is a simple but elegant ranch in the Missouri Breaks, seemingly a million miles from civilization. The modest home she shares with her husband, Sandy Barclay, was built in 1953 by her dad. It has no electricity. A gravity-flow system supplies them with some of the best water in Garfield County from a nearby spring. In addition to their livestock, Leah and Sandy raise a few chickens to see them through emergencies when rain or snow turns Haxby Road to gumbo.

"I figure if you've got three squares a day and a shirt on your back, you're doing okay," she said. "You can't wear more than one shirt at a time anyway."

Shifting into low as she guided her "outfit" through coulees and breaks, and sighting antelope she seemed to know by name, she added: "If I were a millionaire, I'd do just what I'm doing. So I guess I'm a millionaire."

Fred Deigert, M.D., Billings (formerly of Michigan):

"I used to think you had to have trees where you live. But pretty soon, you start seeing sunrises, sunsets and incredible skyscapes."

Right: *Garfield County "outfit."*
Below: *Rodeo acrobatics at the annual Miles City Bucking Horse Sale.*

MICHAEL CRUMMETT PHOTOS BOTH PAGES

MICHAEL CRUMMETT PHOTOS

Above: *Roundup-area rancher Bob Tully checks a newborn calf.*
Top: *One way to round up a renegade cow is to kidnap her calf.*
Left: *Cowboy Vern Mehr clowns around in the chutes at the Grapevine Ranch near Ft. Smith.*

Look for Elaine Corrigan, Lois Crepeau or the other members of Wednesday's Outdoor Women in Missoula on any day but Wednesday. That is their day away from the city, their jobs, their kids and their men. Come rain or shine, Christmas or New Year's, it is their day to be outdoors. In the summer, they can be found hiking as close to home as the Rattlesnake Wilderness or as far away as the Bob Marshall. In the winter, chances are they will be practicing telemark turns on top of Lolo Pass.

There are no rules or requirements for membership in Wednesday's Outdoor Women. A love of the outdoors is the tie that binds these 20 to 25 women across distinctions that would keep them apart in town. Some work; some do not. Some are married; some aren't. Some are in their 40s, some in their 70s. About the only requirement is to show up in the K-Mart parking lot with gear and a sack lunch at 9 a.m. on Wednesday. Logistics are figured out on the spot, and usually within an hour, the "WOW girls" are doing what they like best— hiking or skiing in the environment that keeps them firmly attached to their Western Montana home.

NORMA TIRRELL

Above: *Come rain or shine, Christmas or New Year's, if it's Wednesday, the "WOW girls" are together outdoors.*
Below: *Conservation educator Vince Yannone delights Montana audiences with his knowledge of the natural world.*

Judging from his calendar, you would think he was a rock star or the G. Gordon Liddy of Montana's lecture circuit. In fact, he is a biologist. Vince Yannone is a conservation educator for the Montana Department of Fish, Wildlife and Parks, and Montanans can't get enough of him. Performing for about 5,000 people a month, Yannone is booked at least six months in advance and spends an average of three days a week on the road.

A regular on Dick Clark's "American Bandstand" when he was a teenager growing up in Philadelphia, Yannone is a showman in his own right. But his friends usually steal the show: a golden eagle that lost its wings to a live utility wire; a great horned owl that has been grounded by a calcium deposit in a broken wing; a raven that was used for target practice. Many will recover and be released; the ones that will never make it on their own again will become permanent residents in Yannone's backyard south of Helena.

MICHAEL CRUMMETT

Using falconers' gloves to blunt their swordlike talons, Yannone is perfectly at ease with these wild creatures. To the delight of his grade school audiences, he squawks at his companions and ducks jabs from their outstretched wings. Pointing out feather patterns and bone structures that make them unique, he conveys an infectious sense of awe and enthusiasm for the natural world. The show is a natural for Montana audiences because, in Yannone's words, "Montana is an outdoor state." Ticking off a list of doctors and dentists he knows personally, Yannone added: "People give up good-paying jobs to live here because they like the lifstyle. They like to hunt and fish."

Tom Coston, retired regional forester, USFS Northern Region, Missoula:

"Every time I've come home from a trip back East, I've noticed that when you fly over the Mississippi River, the looks of the land change. So does my mind."

MICHAEL CRUMMETT

Sister Clare Hartmann has taught school at St. Paul's Mission on the Fort Belknap Indian Reservation for 49 years: "The Lord didn't want me in China."

He borrows department statistics to prove it. "Seventy-five percent of all Montanans fish or engage in some form of outdoor recreation," he said, "and thirty percent hunt big game or upland game. About one hundred thousand people—nearly one eighth of the state—put in for deer and elk every year."

At the core of every Vince Yannone show is a message to Montanans that the birds and trout and elk they hold so dear are no more certain than Montana's commitment to preserve and protect wildlife habitat.

Raising a golden eagle high above the heads of his audience, Yannone closes the show: "We can't duplicate one of these. We can't duplicate a river drainage. We can't duplicate a wilderness."

"We generally stay in one place three or four years and then move on," said Sister M. Clare Hartmann, a Franciscan sister and teacher at St. Paul's Mission on the Fort Belknap Reservation. "They move us around like pieces on a chessboard."

But Sister Clare has been an exception to the rule of her community, the Milwaukee-based School Sisters of St. Francis. For 49 years, she has taught science to Gros Ventre youngsters on the isolated plains of Northeastern Montana. "We're in the world and not of it, you know; we're not supposed to make any attachments," said the diminutive Sister Clare. "But to tell the truth, I just love it here."

Sister Clare tosses her head back and laughs when she thinks back on the course her life took after she took her vows of poverty, chastity and obedience: "My idea was to go to China. I thought it would be a wonderful place to go and teach those people religion. But they sent me to Hays, instead, and I've been here ever since. The Lord didn't want me in China. This is my China."

To the Gros Ventre people, Sister Clare is "Speaks Holy," one of only a few non-Indians who has been allowed to touch the Sacred Pipe. And to her, the Indians are a lovable, happy and generous people. "The Indian to me is sincere, not false" she said. "When these Indians are your friends, they are your friends."

To her, the Indian is also deeply spiritual. She sees no conflict between Catholicism and Indian spiritual beliefs; she views them, instead, as parallel paths along the same journey. "We use rosary beads to count our prayers," she said. "The Indian uses a pipe to pray to God. We both have our sacraments and rituals."

For years, Sister Clare took her science classes on field trips to the top of nearby Star Hill to search for fossils. But a couple of fires at the mission and too many dances and celebrations where Indians smoked heavily left Sister Clare with a diagnosis of emphysema, and she has abandoned her treks to the top of Star Hill. Down below, there is still plenty of work to be done. Sister Clare is also the school librarian. To raise money for books and other furnishings, she and the other teachers sell used clothing in the basement of the mission. At the end of the 1988 school year, she was about a fifth of the way toward collecting 975,000 soup-can labels to buy a van for the mission school. She was also on her way to the Mother House in Milwaukee, where she would celebrate her 60th jubilee. And in the fall, she would return to Hays for her 50th year with the Gros Ventre.

Venus Bardanouve, *Harlem:*
"You have to value people as the main thing when you live up here."

Right: *Greeting from the Northern Cheyenne Indian Reservation.*
Below: *Winter on the Hi-Line.*

MICHAEL CRUMMETT PHOTOS

Dillon native Steve Banning turned down jobs in Colorado and Alaska to come back home as general manager of the Pegasus Gold Corporation's Zortman-Landusky gold mining project.

Butte native Bill Robinson worked in Los Angeles before returning home to a job with the Western Energy Company. Of his homecoming, he said: "It's like finding your life again."

Every evening when he gets home from work, Bill Banning and his wife, Linda, steal a half-hour from their day to drive up the road from their Clancy home and soak up the quiet beauty of the Helena National Forest. It is their time together, away from the kids and away from Bill's around-the-clock responsibilities as mill manager of the Montana Tunnels Project, a new metals mine south of Helena. A Dillon native and 1966 graduate of the College of Mineral Science and Technology (Montana Tech), Bill is back home after a 20-year mining career that has taken him to Arizona, New Mexico and Colorado. Linda, also from Dillon, said she and her husband have never been happier.

"I've never seen Bill work so hard, and I've never seen him so happy," she said. "They call him in the middle of the night, and he's glad to hear from them. It's just so good to be home."

About 300 miles to the northeast, in the historic mining town of Zortman, Bill's brother, Steve, works as general manager of the state's largest heap-leach gold mine. After graduating from Montana Tech in 1973, he worked at mines in Idaho, Utah, Florida and California before turning down job offers in Colorado and Alaska to come back home.

From his sixth-floor office in uptown Butte, Bill Robinson looks out on the old Steward Mine, where he worked seven years as a shift boss for the Anaconda Company before transferring to Nevada. When the copper market "went to heck," he took a job with Getty Oil in Los Angeles. He laughs, thinking back to the day in 1980 when he decided it was time to get back home: "We were having an earthquake in Los Angeles. I worked on the 19th floor of an office building. I could feel the building swaying, but no one was even talking about it. Someone told me not to worry because the building was earthquake-proof. I couldn't see out the window because of the smog. Just then I got a call from an old Tech buddy who was working in Seattle. He said he was unhappy in Seattle and asked how I was enjoying Los Angeles." Both had heard that things were picking up in Montana and decided to investigate. Robinson got a job with Western Energy in Butte, where he is now vice president of the metals division, and his friend found work at Colstrip. Of his homecoming, this Butte native said simply: "It's like finding your life again."

From Troy to Columbus, Zortman to Whitehall, a resurgence of precious metals mining is bringing home the "kids" who left 10, 15 or 20 years ago with their mining and metallurgical degrees from Montana Tech. Ten years ago, there were 490 Tech grads living in Montana; today there are more than 1,100.

Ten years ago, gold was selling for $35 an ounce; in 1988, it was up to $400 and climbing. That dramatic price increase, combined with new technology that makes it profitable for the first time to extract hard metals from

MICHAEL CRUMMETT PHOTOS BOTH PAGES

Bill Banning is back home after a 20-year mining career that has taken him to Arizona, New Mexico and Colorado. He is the mill manager at the Montana Tunnels Project south of Helena.

Montana's low-grade deposits, has brought about the biggest gold rush since the 1860s. The current boom hasn't reached the height of activity generated by the Anaconda Company in terms of either employment or tax receipts, but it has brought a level of diversification and stability that never was possible with the monolithic Anaconda Company.

"The difference lies in the number of small companies exploring and operating in Montana right now," explained Montana Tech's research and alumni director, Dr. Henry McClernan. "And they're still coming."

"We talk about the boom and bust of Montana's mining history," he added, "but I see this thing playing out for quite a while."

4

LIVING ON THE EDGE IN MONTANA

Our numbers are diminishing. Per capita income is in decline. Record numbers of unemployed workers and college graduates are leaving the state. In remote areas of Central and Eastern Montana, it is hard to attract and keep doctors and teachers. Face it, it is hard to find someone to talk to in a state that boasts four times more cattle than people.

No one ever said it was easy to live in Montana, and therein lies much of its appeal. That fewer than one million people are scattered over 94 million acres is just fine with most Montanans. That ratio inspired newspaperman-historian Joseph Kinsey Howard's description of Montana as a place with "room to swing my arms and to swing my mind."

Montanans treasure their space and take pride in living on the edge: In chancing this year's income against a late-summer hailstorm or an equally unpredictable federal farm policy; in relying on a Piper Cub instead of a company car; in accepting a teaching position 22 miles from the nearest paved road, or in trekking across the Beartooth Mountains in February.

We Montanans have become a source of fascination, if not protracted study, by academicians and Pentagon strategists who generally view Montana as a wasteland and its residents as expendable. After studying the demographics and the rainfall, they conclude that Montana is not fit for human habitation but they cannot agree on Montana's highest and best use. Would our state best serve the nation as a missile range, a toxic waste dump or a national park?

None of the above, in the minds of the one third of one percent of the U.S. population who remain in Montana and wouldn't trade it for the rest of the world.

Call it a shakeout, a squeeze-out or a restructuring. Whatever the name, the changes in Montana's farm economy over the past five years have been dramatic. Inflation, reduced exports, unpredictable farm policies, declining land values, high debt-to-asset ratios, drought and grasshoppers ganged up on Montana farmers and ranchers in the 1980s to produce the worst extended agricultural recession since the Depression. A recent turnaround in prices has brought out the inherent optimism in some observers, who predict it cannot get any worse.

A winter camping trip in the Beartooth Mountains.

RICK GRAETZ

April Milroy, *Garfield County Commissioner, on the subject of distances in Eastern Montana:*

"Until people started pointing them out, we didn't think anything of it. We thought it was normal."

Going with the flow on U.S. 2. MICHAEL CRUMMETT

"The ones who survive this thing are really going to be survivors," said Jim Hanson, president of the First Security Bank in Malta. A former dairy farmer from North Dakota, Hanson got into the banking business when a bad back forced him out of farming. "I've been on that side of the desk," he said from the lender's side. "I know what it's like to be a borrower."

In trying to assess the risk involved in farming and ranching, Hanson keeps coming back to the closest analogy he can think of—a hand of poker: "As an independent bank, we can ride along with our customers a little longer because we know them personally, but when they run out of chips, we have to tell them it's time to fold."

Malta banker Jim Hanson compares farming and ranching with a hand of poker: When borrowers "run out of chips, we have to tell them it's time to fold."

MICHAEL CRUMMETT

Risky as their business may be, Montana farmers and ranchers are rock-solid. Unless they got in at the wrong time or grew too fast, many have been able to weather the storm by tightening their belts. Offsetting the risk in Phillips County is the fact that "we've got good cattle up here," according to Hanson. "Good grass, good breeding and good stockmen."

Hanson equates the impact of a drought or low prices on an agricultural community to the loss of a job in a two-earner household or to the shutdown of a smelter in a company town. A rancher may be able to put off buying a new car, but the local car dealer can't put off his monthly loan payment. Due to this ripple effect, Hanson accepts the fact that he, too, is in the risk business. "You can't take it internally, or it will eat you up," he said. "There are no guarantees that this bank will make money, either."

His statement illustrates the fact that in a changing economy, no one is immune to change, including the banker. In 1980, banks employed roughly 6,000 people in Montana. By 1988, the number had dropped to 4,000, and bank observers say the numbers are still tumbling. A sluggish economy is just part of the picture. Changing technology, mergers and competition from other financial institutions are transforming the banking industry nationwide.

Jim Hanson, banker, Malta:
"If you had a windfall and got a million bucks, would you buy a ranch? No, that's not most people's idea of how to make money."

In Montana, management problems and a changing corporate profile on the part of the regional banks that serve Montana have contributed to the closure or sale of half a dozen banks in rural Montana communities over the past two to three years.

First State Bank of Fort Benton is one of the survivors of a system-wide downsizing begun in 1985 by the Minneapolis-based First Banks System. Formerly a member in good standing of the First Banks family, the Fort Benton bank became an orphan in 1985, when First Banks unloaded some of its smaller banks in a move toward centralization. Bank President Harold Brown, who had also served as president when the bank belonged to First Banks, remembers the day clearly. He had driven to Great Falls for what he thought was a routine meeting at regional headquarters. There, he learned that First Banks had decided to sell its Montana banks in Fort Benton, Lewistown, Forsyth and Livingston.

"It took me about the time it takes to drive from Great Falls to Fort Benton

JOHN REDDY

Above: *Crop dusting near Fort Benton.*
Right: *Malta is a friendly target.*

MICHAEL CRUMMETT

Fort Benton's First Bank became an orphan when the Minneapolis-based First Banks System unloaded some of its smaller banks. President Harold Brown saw it as the opportunity of a lifetime.

Rural Garfield County teacher Barbara Koontz had nine students in 1988, ranging from kindergarten through eighth grade.

to get over the shock," he said. "Then I began to see it as the kind of opportunity that comes along once in a lifetime."

Right away, Brown and the other officers and directors of the bank started putting together a group of local investors to buy the bank. By March 1987, they had accomplished their goal and reopened as an independent bank. Raised on a ranch in Montana's southeast corner, Brown is a quiet man who forms a statement in his mind before he releases it. But he can't hide his pleasure in gaining control of the day-to-day operations and management of the bank. He thinks the change has been good for the community, too.

"We're better able to service our community now because we can respond to local needs," he said. "If a customer can satisfy us where things are [financially], we don't have to regurgitate it to the hierarchy and wait for the hierarchy to get back to us."

The Montana economy has produced its share of detractors and expatriates over the past few years, but Harold Brown is not among them. "We can be negative about the ag economy we've been going through," he said, "but there are lots of opportunities here, too." He insists that business can make it in this economy, and added: "The ones that succeed will be the ones that provide good, solid service to their market area."

Last February, a snowstorm took the roof off Barbara Koontz's teacherage, an otherwise cozy log cabin that sits behind the one-room Benzien School in Garfield County. She was without electricity for four days. But that was nothing compared with the year before, when the well froze at Billup School in Powder River County. Neighboring ranchers hauled water to her for three weeks.

"You've got to look at it as an adventure," said Koontz, who has been teaching in rural schools in Nevada and Montana for the past 10 years. "All the teachers I know have had run-ins with rattlesnakes and skunks. It just goes with the territory."

Benzien School is 15 miles north of Sand Springs and 150 miles from her home in Ryegate, where Koontz spends weekends with her husband, a retired schoolteacher. It sounds isolated but, again, it's nothing compared with Billup School, which she describes as "50 miles from anywhere you'd want to be."

Beyond the isolation, there is the matter of pay, which is notoriously low for rural schoolteachers. While rural school boards are not known for their generosity, compensation comes in other ways—an occasional dinner with students and their families, half a beef for the freezer, free household repairs. More important are the non-monetary rewards that keep Montana's 110 rural, one-room schools supplied with teachers.

Above: *Rural kids have a greater sense of responsibility than city kids, according to Benzien School teacher Koontz.*
Right: *Picking up the mail before school gets started.*

A cool February sun lingers over the Terry Badlands.

"The kids are super," said Koontz, who taught school in Las Vegas before moving to Montana. "Rural kids have a greater sense of responsibility than city kids. They dig in and do their work, and if there are any problems, the parents are right there."

Koontz is drawn as much to the prairie as she is to the people of Eastern Montana. "I'm an avid walker," she said. "Every day after work, I take about a 30-minute walk. I love the sunrises and sunsets out here, and the fresh air is a joy."

She hasn't given a lot of thought to what it takes to be a rural school-teacher because to her, it comes naturally. But at the top of her list would be the ability to "take things in stride," to be self-sufficient and easy-going. "I look to spend the rest of my teaching career in rural schools," she said.

Often it happens during the first snowstorm of the season, or the last. Often, it is right before big-game season, when over-eager hunters take to the sky in search of game. Too often, an airplane accident is the result of a foolish decision.

These are the observations of state aviation officials whose job it is to find aircraft that get into trouble, generally over the rugged mountains of Western Montana. "We're high on the list of states where airplanes go down," said State Aeronautics Commissioner Mike Ferguson. He observed that most crash victims are nonresidents who are "totally inexperienced in mountain

The aeronautics commission has 14 volunteer district search coordinators, most of whom are fixed base operators around the state. One of the busiest is Mike Strand, owner of Kalispell's Strand Aviation. Strand flew for the Army for 12 years before opening his aviation business in Kalispell in 1965. An experienced mountain pilot, he averages a couple of searches a year.

flying." Just to set the record straight, however, he points out that aviation is still one of the safest ways to get around. Between January 1, 1986 and March 31, 1988, 38 people died in airplane accidents in Montana, compared with 487 highway fatalities.

With 4,000 pilots and just less than 3,000 private airplanes, Montana is second only to Alaska in per capita ownership of aircraft. Because this sprawling state is so dependent on general aviation, the aeronautics commission has developed an unusual safety clinic to train pilots in mountain search operations. The only one of its kind in the nation, the Mountain Search Pilot Clinic takes place every September in an area that has been referred to by some pilots as the "Bermuda Triangle" of general aviation—the mountainous area between Kalispell and the Continental Divide.

Flying in and out of back-country airstrips at Spotted Bear, Meadow Gorge and Schafer Meadows, about 30 pilots put in a weekend of time at their expense learning how to conduct contour searches over the mountains, spot crash sites and make crash landings. Each year, there are more applicants for the clinic than there are openings. Once they become certified as mountain search pilots, they join one of the largest volunteer search pilot networks in the nation. At any given time, 1,500 pilots are on call in Montana to help conduct searches. Nearly 300 have been certified by the clinic.

You can ask a dozen pilots why they put themselves through it but their answers are all variations on one theme: "You could be the one they're looking for," said Guy Willson of Moore, one of last year's clinic participants. "I'd like to know that someone is looking for me if I go down," echoed Rob McDowell of Cardwell.

It has been said that Helena is the worst place to gauge a political campaign because residents of the capital city are so wrapped up in government that they are out of touch with the rest of the state. Arguably, Plentywood and Ekalaka are even further removed. Relying on Williston, North Dakota, and Rapid City, South Dakota,for television news, the residents of these and other Eastern Montana communities are why many people think Montana would make more sense as two states, not one. "We know more about South Dakota politics than we do about Montana," said Ekalaka veterinarian Greg Tooke. "The people in this area think they might as well be residents of South Dakota."

House calls are so far apart in Carter County that Ekalaka veterinarian Greg Tooke relies on his small, single-engine airplane to conduct much of his business

Canadian bar traffic keeps Montana Highway Patrolman Del Kranzler busy in Montana's extreme northeast corner.

Ekalaka is literally the end of the line, marking the terminus of State Highway 7. There is so little pavement in Carter County that Tooke relies on his small, single-engine airplane for much of his business. Even so, he figures he puts 15,000 to 20,000 miles on his pickup each year.

Plenty of browse plus protein-rich buffalo grass and wheatgrass make Carter County a good place to raise sheep and cattle and, therefore, a good place to practice veterinary medicine. Tooke returned to his native Carter County after graduating from veterinary school 15 years ago and has practiced there ever since. Carter County has not been successful with medical doctors. A member of the Ekalaka Hospital Board, Tooke said Ekalaka has seen six doctors come and go in three years. "The novelty of this place wears off quickly if you weren't raised here," he said.

As a native, however, Tooke can't think of any place he'd rather be. Taking longer than he thought it would to find his brother and ranch partner, Garth, who is said to be trailing cows somewhere south of the Powderville Road, he contemplated his attachment to this lonely land and concluded that the pace of life in Carter County is a good part of its appeal.

"In this country, scheduling is pretty much unheard of," he said. "There's a rancher wants me to take a look at one of his bulls this afternoon. Not at one o'clock, just sometime this afternoon. I'll make it."

Farther north, the pace picks up a little for Del Kranzler, a Montana Highway Patrolman based in Plentywood. Kranzler patrols Montana's extreme northeast corner, from the North Dakota border to the Valley County line, and from Montana's border with Saskatchewan to the northern edge of Roosevelt County. It may be two weeks before Kranzler sees another highway patrolman along the route, but hardly a day passes when he does not have business with the border patrol agents at the Port of Raymond, Montana's second-busiest border crossing.

"We get quite a little bar traffic," said Kranzler, as he explained the southern migration of Canadians to Montana and North Dakota, especially on weekends. "Canadians come down here to drink and gamble," he said. "The drinking laws in Canada aren't as strict as they were when I first started working here, but Canadians still can't drink on Sundays."

That is good news for Plentywood, a community of 2,600 people and nine bars. Each year, the community takes in about $1 million in Canadian currency, relying heavily on its northern neighbors to diversify an agriculture- and oil-based economy.

As long as the laws don't change north of the border, neither will the traffic on this side. Said one customs agent: "Canadians think nothing of driving a hundred miles in a blizzard for a case of beer."

Winter is a critical time for Montana's livestock producers. **Above:** These Garfield County bulls have just come through a blizzard. **Right:** Stillwater rancher Bill Mackay, Jr., gets an early start on winter feeding.

T om Stanton sees his family for maybe an hour or two, three or four times a month. That is generally on Sunday, when he drives into town for church. The rest of the time, he is out at the ranch, near Brusett. Claudia and the kids live in Jordan, where she works as matron of Montana's only public high school dormitory. The kids go to school in town and live with their mother in the dorm.

"The farm crunch really put us in a bind, so Claudia took a job in town three years ago," said Tom as he lingered over one more cup of coffee with his wife before driving back to the ranch. "I felt like I was going through a divorce when she and the kids left."

MICHAEL CRUMMETT PHOTOS BOTH PAGES

If they're lucky, Claudia and Tom Stanton see each other once a week. She took a job in town as matron of the Garfield County High School dormitory to make ends meet. He holds down a ranch near Brusett that has been in the Stanton family for three generations.

It has been a strain on the whole family, but one they accept as necessary and temporary. Claudia predicts she will have to spend at least one more year in town because "we've had another dry year, so it doesn't look too good for our crops."

The dormitory has been separating Garfield County families for more than 50 years. As hard as it is on both kids and parents, it beats busing kids up to 120 miles round-trip every day. "It didn't seem so bad as a kid," Tom remembered of the two years he lived in the dorm while going to school in town.

"Actually, it can be kind of fun for the kids," Claudia added. "It's like having twenty-three brothers and sisters."

Claudia's day begins at 6:30 a.m. with breakfast for her charges and ends when the last one goes down at night. During the day, she cooks and cleans, plans menus and buys groceries. On special occasions, she arranges an evening of pizza and videos for the kids. "I'd like to be bored for about three weeks," she said. "I'd lock myself into a room with my sewing machine and get some work done."

The Stantons are no different from any other farm or ranch family, doing what they have to do to get by. "At least, we're only twenty-three miles apart," Claudia said of her temporary separation from her husband.

Tom borrows strength from two earlier generations of Stantons. "My folks and grandfolks had similar problems out here, and they survived it," he said. "So will we and so will our kids."

J oannie Sun is one of those bright, college-bound students who find it so difficult to stay in Montana once they have learned specialized skills that don't match Montana job descriptions. This fall she enrolled in the School of Biomedical Engineering at Duke University but hopes to return to Montana someday, either as a college professor or a medical doctor.

A graduate of Bozeman Senior High School, she moved to Montana with her family in 1978, and has lived here long enough to get attached and call it home. "I've always felt lucky to live in Bozeman," she said. "It has such a good high school. And the library at MSU [Montana State University] is great for research."

Joannie's parents, both professors at MSU, were born and raised in Taiwan. "Education was everything to my parents when they were growing up," said Joannie. "They've relaxed a lot about grades with me and my brother, but their instinct is still to get a strong education."

We Montanans

Spring storm brewing over the Little Belt Mountains.

The combination of MSU and a strong public school system brought the Suns to Bozeman. "My parents checked out schools very carefully when they decided to leave Michigan," she said. "They chose Bozeman because they thought we could get a good education here."

If Joannie's high school achievements are a measure, they made the right choice. In June, she was one of two state finalists to compete in a national student congress sponsored by the National Forensics League. The year before, she was a delegate to Girls' Nation in Washington, D.C.

"I got started in public speaking because I thought it was important, but then it got to be fun," she said. Joannie enjoys matching wits with an adversary under pressure. "It's fun because you're always up against someone with an opposing idea."

As much as she enjoys politics and debate, she doesn't envision a career in public affairs. "I'll probably do something that's math- or science-related," she said. "The career I choose must be flexible so that I can live where I want to live. Someday I'd like to come back to Montana, but I'd like to try a big city first."

Bozeman High School graduate Joannie Sun is studying at Duke University, where she is learning specialized skills that may not match a Montana job description when she graduates.

Most rural Montanans wouldn't trade their lifestyle for 10 shopping malls, but a hospital would be nice. It's unnerving to live 110 miles from the nearest medical center, half that distance on gravel. It is also a way of life in the kind of community that can't keep a doctor but supports a healthy veterinary practice. Rural Montanans have been putting up with it for years, but some have devised ingenious ways of closing the medical gap.

Every year the Northeastern Montana Medical Society, which consists of about 20 doctors from Valley, Roosevelt, Daniels and Sheridan counties, hosts a continuing-education course that would be the envy of any respectable group practice. Specialists from some of the nation's leading medical centers pay their way to spend a day at the Fort Peck Hotel, updating their rural colleagues on the latest developments in medical research and surgical techniques.

"Our biggest catch is Dr. E. Donnall Thomas, the most eminent bone marrow transplant specialist in the United States," said Dr. Mark Listerud, a Wolf Point surgeon who serves as program chairman for the annual event. Other speakers include leading hematologists, oncologists, plastic surgeons and cardiac surgeons.

According to Dr. Listerud, the timing of the annual event is critical. "We've been holding these meetings for the past 20 or 25 years, on or around the last day of October," he said. "That's when the season is open for deer, antelope and upland game, and that's the bait that gets our guests out here."

"We invite four or five doctors each year," he explained. "The ones who want to hunt deer and antelope generally come two or three days early. We have lectures all day Saturday and spend Sunday and Monday hunting birds."

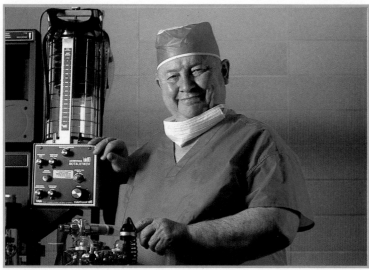

MICHAEL CRUMMETT PHOTOS

Wolf Point general surgeon Dr. Mark Listerud and his colleagues have developed an ingenious continuing education program for Northeastern Montana.

According to Dr. Listerud, there is plenty of community support for the event. Farmers and ranchers open their land to the visiting physicians, and members of the Northeastern Montana Medical Society serve as guides.

Dr. Listerud has been practicing surgery in his native Wolf Point for 30 years. It is his opinion that Montana's relative isolation does not have to be

Upland birds and big game hunting are the bait that attracts some of the nation's leading medical specialists to Fort Peck every fall.

Dan Muniak, physician's assistant, is part of an evolving profession in Montana and other rural areas that cannot attract and hold doctors.

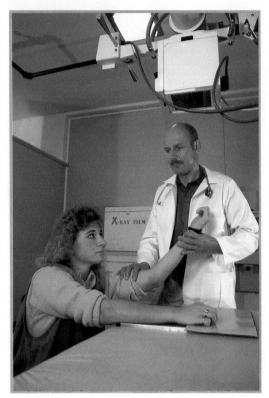

T.J. Gilles, *newspaperman, Great Falls:*

"In the real bad moments, living in Montana has almost been a socio-economic version of advice given to soldiers about to assault a beachhead in World War II: 'Look at the guy on your right. Chances are, he won't be here when we get through this."

a handicap: "It ain't where you are; it's what's going on behind your eyeballs that counts. If you want to keep current with your profession, you can do it from as remote a place as Wolf Point."

More remote than Wolf Point is Jordan, where the folks gave up looking for a physician and are grateful for a physician assistant. Dan Muniak, P.A., does just about everything an M.D. does except write prescriptions and perform major surgery. As a physician assistant, he has been academically and clinically trained to provide primary patient care under the sponsorship of a licensed physician. In most cases, that means the M.D. and P.A. work together as a team. In Garfield County, it means that Muniak's sponsoring physicians are 85 miles down the road in Miles City.

It's an evolving profession in Montana, according to Muniak, but one that is well established nationally. In 1987, roughly 16,000 physician assistants were employed by physicians and institutions nationally. In Montana, there are only 17. State laws and regulations governing physician assistants are more stringent in Montana than in many other states, and that is a disadvantage in a rural state, in Muniak's view. He points out that neighboring South Dakota, with fewer residents, has about 150 physician assistants.

Like so many rural communities, Jordan has neither economic nor cultural appeal to most physicians, but for Dan Muniak and his wife, Paula, Jordan is just right. Raised in Massachusetts, the Muniaks have been Westerners since 1967. They like Jordan for different reasons, Paula because she thinks a small, close-knit community is a great place to raise kids, and Dan because he knows it is a great place to hunt antelope. "I'm on call all of the time," he said, "but I have an understanding with the community about antelope season."

Muniak knows all about the romance of rural health care, having gained fame in South Dakota, where he delivered a baby by phone during a blizzard. But he said rural health care has changed dramatically since the days of the country doctor.

"It used to be that you did what you could for a patient; now, we're practicing legal medicine," he said. "Even if you live in Jordan, you have to deliver the same standard of care they're getting in Seattle."

Rural decay. MICHAEL CRUMMETT PHOTOS

MICHAEL CRUMMETT

JOHN REDDY

NORMA TIRRELL

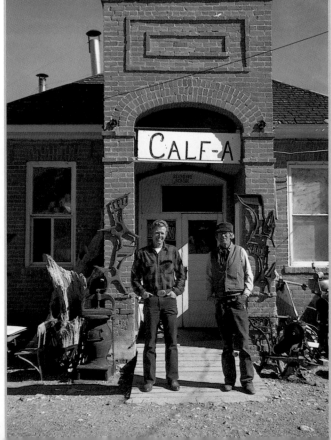

Above: *Montana skyline.*
Top: *Kids and horses were made for each other.*
Right: *Homemade donuts, rolls and soup draw locals and truckers alike to Yesterday's Calf-A, on Interstate 15 south of Dillon.*

5

THE SEASONS AND EVENTS
OF OUR LIVES

A cattleman's year begins on payday, sometime during the fall shipping season. A fly fisherman lives for spring's first mayfly hatch. For traditionalist Plains Indians, summer is a time of spiritual renewal through a ceremony called the Sun Dance. A hunter rejoices in autumn's first snow. And in November, skiers are warming up for their favorite season when other Montanans are packing to leave or wishing they could. Those who stick around view the months of January, February and March not as winter but as basketball season—something to do between harvest and seeding.

A calendar may be a good way to keep track of birthdays and anniversaries, but it has little to do with the cycle of life in Montana. We Montanans do not fit neatly into the boxes and squares that divide the Gregorian calendar. We live from season to season, with events like spring branding or the arrival of the first meadowlark or the opening day of big-game season as the mileposts against which we measure progress or change from one year to the next.

The northern climate that scares so many people away from Montana is the glue that keeps the rest of us here. While some of us merely endure winter, we accept it as the price of four gloriously distinct seasons. Each has its rituals, each has its "firsts"—the first daffodil, the first trout, the first lamb, the first vine-ripened tomato, the first overhead clatter of migrating honkers, the first snow.

From summer solstice parties to winter parades, we have devised dozens of excuses for getting together to celebrate the seasons. These are the events that shape our year. These are the red-letter days on our calendar.

TIM CHRISTIE

Fall is the best time of the year for Montana's big-game hunters.

For students, it is a day to drink some beers, see how many of their friends they can squeeze into a VW bus and generally hang out in the stadium parking lot. For alumni, it is a marathon tailgate party—a day to drink some beers, see old friends and relive some of the best years of their lives. For players, the annual Bobcat-Grizzly game is hell. The whole season hangs on the next two hours. It has been going on since 1897, making the annual contest between Montana State University and the University of Montana one of the oldest intercollegiate rivalries west of the Mississippi. In 1987, it drew more than 17,000 fans, making MSU's Reno H. Sales Stadium the seventh-largest city in Montana—for one day.

In 1987, the Bobcat-Grizzly game **(top)** drew more than 17,000 fans, making Montana State University's Reno H. Sales Stadium the seventh-largest city in Montana for one day.

Above and right: For students, it's a day to drink beer and hang out in the stadium parking lot.

I kiss him goodbye the first of September and kiss him hello the first of December," said Debbie Chatlain of her husband, Denny. While many seasonal workers are between jobs, Denny and Montana's other 595 licensed outfitters are hitting the peak of their season. The Chatlains, both natives of Valier, guide hunters to bear, elk and deer in the Beartooth Mountains above

MICHAEL CRUMMETT

Red Lodge. For seven years, they packed into the northern tip of the Bob Marshall Wilderness, west of Dupuyer. But in 1986, they abandoned the Bob because, in their opinion, it was getting too crowded.

Every year, Montana sells hunting licenses to 33,000 non-residents. By comparison, an estimated 218,000 resident hunters purchase licenses. Hunting is big business in Montana. Outfitters alone estimate that their industry is worth $35 million a year in direct expenditures.

It is the nonresidents who rely on outfitters and guides to provide them with a hunting experience in unfamiliar territory. Some come back year after year to hunt with the same outfitter; for some, a guided hunt in Montana's game-rich back country is the experience of a lifetime.

Denny Chatlain is one of nearly 600 licensed outfitters in the state who make a living by guiding hunters—mostly nonresidents—into Montana's game-rich back country.

T.J. Gilles, newspaperman, Great Falls:

"The nights are getting cool, gardeners and farmers are keeping an eye on the thermometer and an ear on the radio weather report for warning of the first frost, the wood haulers are in a frenzy and the unsubtle signs everywhere tell us that summer's about over."

After their ostentatious show of color and fragrance in early May, Flathead Lake's cherry orchards settle down to the serious business of producing some of the nation's plumpest, sweetest cherries in June and July.

Less visible but gaining strength in their eighth year are a hundred acres of apples tucked behind some low hills at the south end of the lake, near Polson. About 30,000 trees have reached various stages of maturity and are now producing truckloads of Macintosh and Delicious apples that are marketed in Montana and throughout the West.

If the climate around Flathead Lake works for cherries, why not apples? That was the thinking of Dave Drum, an entrepreneur who moved to Polson from Billings in 1974 to retire. Never one to let a good idea lie idle, Drum began learning everything there was to know about apples until 1978, when he "started getting really excited about apples."

By 1980, his son, Dan, had several orchards planted and is now experimenting with pears, peaches and apricots. Dave works out of a small office in Polson, hustling new markets and developing new orchards. By getting more people interested in growing apples, he hopes to expand production to a level that will justify a processing plant for both apples and cherries. He envisions the day when trucks leaving the Flathead Valley will be hauling not just boxes of fresh fruit but cans of pie filling and applesauce as well. Ambitious, perhaps, but not surprising from the man who founded a nationwide network of camping facilities that came to be known as Kampgrounds of America.

It would be difficult for Aggie Helle to single out one season as her favorite. With each come the rituals that make farming and ranching such a compelling lifestyle. How do you weigh the expectation of spring against the

Top: *If the Flathead Lake climate works for cherries* (**above**), *entrepreneur Dave Drum thinks it should work for apples, too.*

Right: *Not all is fragrant blossoms and sunshine for Montana's cherry growers. East Shore grower Juanita Rousselle tends to the winter task of pruning her trees.*

MICHAEL CRUMMETT PHOTOS BOTH PAGES

satisfaction of fall? The dawn-to-dark workday of summer against winter's retreat? A second-generation sheep and cattle producer in Beaverhead County, Aggie loves them all.

"Spring is full of hope and excitement," she said, as she enumerated the demands of the season on the diversified farm and ranch operation she runs

with her husband, Joe, their boys, Tom and John, and her brother, Peter Rebish. No sooner is the grain seeded than it is time to start shearing ewes. Lambing runs from May into June, and then the serious work begins. Between moving livestock up to the high country and cutting hay down below, the Helles are moving in so many directions that they rely on two-way radios and a mobile phone to keep track of one another. From time to time between mid-April and the end of October, the Helles hire extra hands to help with lambing, docking, shearing and sorting. Aggie's job is to feed them, and that means driving to sheep camps as much as 75 miles away to prepare and serve home-cooked meals on site.

"It's a lot of work," she said. "But this is a nice life. In the fall, I love to see the sheep coming off the mountain, moving through the quaking aspen," she said. "The lambs are fat coming off the forest, and that's your reward."

Aggie views her world from a beautifully kept house and yard on a rise overlooking the Beaverhead Valley, just north of Dillon. To the west are the Pioneers; to the east, the Ruby Range. On a mild day in late February, the Helles were well into calving season. Between trips to town for supplies and what seemed like an around-the-clock laundry service, Aggie worried about the windows. Winter's residue had begun to obscure her view. Clearly, it was bothering her but she wanted the windows to look nice for Easter, which was another month away. In a weak moment, she confessed that winter does not really measure up to spring, summer and fall. Her world had turned brown and gray, and Aggie said she was ready for green.

For hundreds of Western Montanans, Les and Hanneke Ippisch fulfill a need for Christmas the way it used to be. A visit to their home, northwest of Missoula, is a welcome retreat from the hassle of holiday shopping. A shopping trip to be sure, this one is a pleasure.

About a month before Christmas, Les and Hanneke open their home for their annual Christmas market. Only five days long, the market culminates a year of handcrafted work by the entire Ippisch family. Wooden wildlife toys, candle holders, brightly painted ornaments, delicate wooden snowflakes and angels, even a Montana-style nativity scene, are among the hundreds of one-of-a-kind gifts that disappear in five days.

Much of the appeal of the Ippisches' Christmas market is the setting in which it is held. Just off Ninemile Road, in the woods north of Huson, Les and Hanneke have transformed an old schoolhouse into a storybook home. Originally built by the Anaconda Company for loggers' families, the house is a tasteful blend of bright colors and muted wood tones, with natural light and

Above: *It would be hard for Beaverhead County sheep and cattle producer Aggie Helle to choose her favorite season. She loves them all.* **Facing page:** *Summer is county fair time across Montana—time to visit the kids' barn and time to show off this year's 4-H project.*

Sarah Larson, Collins:
"You don't speak to a man between spring and fall if it doesn't pertain to farming."

the outdoor environment key elements of the design. At Christmas, it just feels good to be there. The fragrance indoors is a mix of pine and fresh-ground coffee. Candles illuminate the nooks and crannies that Les and Hanneke have built into their home — a bedroom loft, a book loft and a bell tower, which is Hanneke's idea of "a lovely place to spin or look at the moon."

"We like to make holes in the walls," said Hanneke, a Dutch native who moved to the United States from Sweden in 1952. She lived in California before moving to Missoula, where she met and married Les. She likes the Huson area because it reminds her of "the Old Country." And area residents are grateful to her for bringing a piece of the Old Country with her to Montana.

Artisans Les and Hanneke Ippisch fulfill a need for Christmas the way it used to be.

Most Montanans have never heard of the town of Collins. It died when the railroad was rerouted through Choteau. But it is still home to a handful of farmers who grow grain in this rich sweep of prairie on the western edge of North-central Montana's Golden Triangle.

Once a year, on a September weekend after harvest, Collins is thoroughly congested with cars heading to the Teton Antique Steam & Gas Threshing Association's annual threshing bee. Ove and Sarah Larson have hosted the bee for nearly a decade. Ove, who is as Norwegian as his name implies, has a thing about steam engines. He collects them and fixes them. He has built a small sawmill to cut the wood that fuels them. Every year, he plants five acres in oats because they work best in his steam-driven threshing machines.

A trip to his farm in September is like a trip back in time. Shocks of grain stand ready for threshing. Case Engines and Red River

For nearly a decade, Collins farmer Ove Larson has hosted the Teton Antique Steam and Gas Engine Association's annual threshing bee in September.

Specials look out of place on a modern farm except for one thing: they work.

Ove has been puttering around with steam engines since he was a kid working as a water tender in southern Minnesota. "So many were scrapped out for metal during World War II," he lamented. "So we try to save as many as we can before they disappear completely." Ove is not alone in his passion for steam engines. Every year, 400 to 500 like-minded Montanans attend the Larson bee, one of about half a dozen in the state. Not all participants are farmers; according to Ove, there is a minister and a lawyer in the Teton association. They may not cross paths for a year. But come September, they travel miles to share their common passion.

Above: *Larry McKenzie, Lewistown, with a 1910 Case steam engine.*
Top: *Shocks of grain await steam-driven threshing machines.*
Right: *Ove Larson gets a hand in setting the belt on his 1912 Case steam engine.*

NORMA TIRRELL PHOTOS

Above: *Claude Tesmer is Glacier National Park's road crew supervisor. It's his job to open Going-to-the-Sun Road in the spring and keep it open through summer.*
Top: *Glacier National Park officials allow tourists to drive up to Logan Pass in early spring to watch the opening of Going-to-the-Sun Road.*

Claude Tesmer does not know where all those tourists come from, but the day he and his crew clear the last snowdrift from Going-to-the-Sun Road, they are there, motoring over one of the most scenic mountain passes in the world. "It's like they just hatch out of the sun," said the Glacier National Park road crew supervisor.

For the past 35 years, Tesmer has been taking care of Montana's beloved Sun Road. Starting as a seasonal laborer in 1953, he is now assistant chief of maintenance for the park. He has watched the park's road maintenance operation grow from "quiet and laid back to hectic" as tourist pressure grows. Since 1933, when the 52-mile, transmountain highway was completed, annual park visitation has grown from 76,000 to 1.6 million.

A steady stream of cars, from early June to mid-October, is just part of the problem of maintaining a road that Tesmer is convinced "would never be built today" due to high costs and environmental considerations. Weather-related closures, rock slides and avalanches compound the job for Tesmer and his crew.

They begin the road-opening operation in mid-March. Normally, by the first of May, they have cleared all but the last 15 miles

Heaven's Peak, Glacier National Park.

JOHN REDDY

across the top of Logan Pass. That stretch, which includes a locally notorious landmark called the "big drift" just east of the pass, generally takes a month. "I've seen the big drift in excess of 70 feet deep," said Tesmer.

Just before the road opened in 1988, a 50-pound boulder peeled away from one of the walls that tower over Sun Road and crashed through the windshield of the truck Tesmer was driving. "All of a sudden, it felt like the pickup exploded and the next thing I knew, there was this boulder beside me," he recalled. It missed Tesmer's head by inches.

It is all part of a memorable career that began at an early age for Tesmer, who grew up on a farm in North Dakota. After graduating from high school, he assumed he would take up farming but decided to have a look at the outside world first. "I was headed for the West Coast, and this is where I ran out of money," he said.

For anyone who views Montana's small farm and ranch communities as isolated outposts that roll up the covers in January and don't come out 'til spring, try finding a parking place within six blocks of a high school gymnasium on a Saturday night in February. It is basketball season, and bleachers from one end of the state to the other are packed. Many of the fans think nothing of driving 100 miles in sub-zero temperatures to catch a good game.

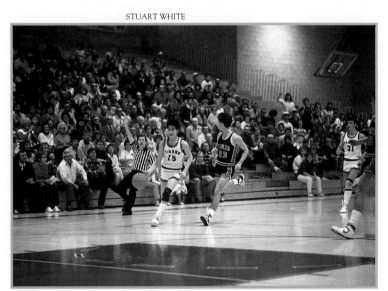

STUART WHITE

More than entertainment, basketball is the social center of gravity in many rural communities, particularly in the eastern part of the state. In Nashua, a good evening of basketball gets under way with the fifth and sixth graders as soon as the sun goes down at 4 p.m; the seventh and eighth graders go on at 5 p.m.; junior varsity starts at 6; and varsity follows at 7:30.

"It's those early games that bring out the grandmas and grandpas," according to Kay Opp, a loyal Nashua Porkies fan. The really hardcore fans—the parents—are in place with buttons, banners and booming voices at the opening tip-off of the varsity game.

After a home game, the action moves from the Nashua High gym to private homes, where friends gather for snacks, a game of Trivial Pursuit or Pictionary and plenty of post-game analysis, or to Bergie's—a downtown drugstore and soda fountain. Proprietor Larry Bergstrom generally has a videotape of the game so that his patrons can re-live it play by play.

Whether a team is at home or on the road, the players can count on their fans to be there. Opheim Vikings starter Paul Shaffer is one of those small, aggressive players who is fun to watch because he is all over the floor at once. A 1988 graduate of Opheim High, he has been playing ball since fifth grade, and it shows. After college, he hopes to settle in Billings—a "nice-sized town"—but he is grateful for the boost he got from Opheim: "It's great to have the whole town behind you when you're playing ball."

Above: *Basketball is the social center of gravity in many rural communities.*
Facing page: *Elk are mong the most treasured of Montana's big-game species.*

CONRAD ROWE

6

KEEPERS & INTERPRETERS OF OUR LIFE IN MONTANA

I t may be hard to find a niche in what newspaper columnist T.J. Gilles describes as the state's "niche-poor economy," but Montana has provided unlimited opportunity to its artists and writers. Since the early part of the century, when Charlie Russell's work began appearing at galleries in London, New York and Chicago, and Americans began developing romantic notions about the West through books written by James Willard Schultz and Frank Bird Linderman, Montana has drawn and nurtured more than its share of distinguished painters, poets, potters, sculptors, novelists, even musicians.

Below: Deer Lodge National Forest. Bottom: Sunset over the Beartooths.

Trying to interpret this phenomenon for a national audience in a 1981 issue of *The New York Times Book Review*, Bozeman writer David Quammen sized up Montana's literary landscape this way: "It has gotten so that when another stranger settles into town with no visible means of support and begins keeping late weekday hours at the Silver Dollar, going about unshaven, making multiple daily trips to the post office, Montana folks can accurately assume that, if he is not a fugitive from the F.B.I. or a remittance man from Boston, he is probably just another harmless writer."

You cannot talk to Montana artists and writers about their craft without some mention of the link between their work and their environment. Mountain valleys that lift their eyes and spirits, prairie landscapes that stretch their imaginations, sunsets that ooze a dozen shades of purple across the sky before giving up, and rivers that still run clear and yield wild trout. These are some of the obvious attractions Montana holds for the creative mind.

But there are other factors, each as fundamental and significant as the size and shape of the land. For one thing, Montana is a cheap place to live, an important consideration for anyone trying to make it in the hungry world of art and literature. Its relative isolation and sparse population have made Montana a good hideout for artists and writers who shun the pace and the priorities of a metropolitan environment. Explaining why Montana writers can't be bothered with the current best-seller, Quammen talks about the "intellectual buffer zone that makes Montana such a wonderful place for contemplation."

JOHN REDDY PHOTOS

You cannot talk to Montana artists and writers about their craft without some mention of the link between their work and their environment. McDonald Creek, Glacier National Park.

JOHN REDDY PHOTOS

Above: *Prairies stretch the imagination.*
Right: *Internationally known sculptor Rudy Autio grew up in Butte and makes his home in Missoula.*

There seems to be greater potential for self-discovery in an environment that encourages participation in the arts and gives artists space to experiment and grow. Describing the transition she made from California homemaker to Montana writer and editor, Bozeman's Ursula Smith explains: "I never would have even tried writing in California. It was so immense, and there was so much talent and action there, I was not aware of my own potential."

For fiber-construction artist Dana Boussard of Arlee, it was the time she spent in the contemporary art scene of New York City and San Francisco that brought into focus the primitive, Western symbols that figure so prominently in her work.

Perhaps most important is the weight of tradition. Ever since early writers like H.G. Merriam were willing to share their time and wisdom with promising young authors like Dorothy Johnson and A.B. Guthrie, Jr., Montana has distinguished itself as a place to learn the craft of writing. Similarly, Montana's early cowboy and landscape artists—the Russells and Paxsons and Seltzers—stirred the imagination not only of a curious, East Coast audience, but also of three generations of artists to follow. Not all have adhered to the Western genre, but many have established themselves in a national market. Potters from all over the world come to study and work together at Helena's Archie Bray Foundation, whose renowned, resident potters and sculptors have included Montanans Peter Voulkos, Rudy Autio and David Shaner.

MICHAEL CRUMMETT

Traditional Blackfeet symbols.

For whatever reason, Montana has cultivated a rich creative community. Its residents are the interpreters of our life in Montana. These are the people who can tell the rest of the world what it is like to grow up in a town like Dupuyer or on the Fort Belknap Indian Reservation. These are the people who can build a delicate vessel from the most basic of elements—earth and fire. These are the people who find significance in a rural ritual like spring lambing, and make it meaningful to the urban world through symbols or statements that have universal appeal.

These artists and writers are closely related to the historians who find significance in the people and events of a very young state. Whether they are published scholars or Indian elders, these Montanans sense the importance of an aging railroader's story, a box of old payroll records from the Anaconda Company or the process by which a hide is tanned and turned into moccasins. These are the keepers and recorders of our life in Montana.

Critics have found it difficult to define Phil Aaberg's music. It is a meld of so many parts—ranging from classical to rock, country to jazz—that Aaberg's fans would swear they have nothing in common. But to Montana listeners, it's easy. Aaberg's solo piano is just-plain-great traveling music.

If you think of U.S. 2 as something merely to endure, try it to the accompaniment of Aaberg's first solo album, "High Plains." Drop the tape

MICHAEL CRUMMETT

Above and right: *The Sweetgrass Hills and the creatures of North-central Montana are the inspiration behind some of Chester native Phil Aaberg's music.*

JOHN REDDY

Phil Aaberg lives in Oakland, California where he writes and records music, but he gets back to Montana as often as possible.

IRENE YOUNG PHOTO,
COURTESY WINDHAM HILL RECORDS

Eric Funk, composer, Bozeman:
"Montana provides me with the clarity I need for my work."

Fabric-construction artist Dana Boussard creates "public space art" using symbols from her Montana home.

MICHAEL CRUMMETT

into the deck at Havre, and before you know it, you are in Shelby. Somewhere in between, you were a freight train, high-balling across the plains in "West-bound." "Sweetgrass" and "Marias River Breakdown" opened your mind to the possibilities of North-central Montana. By the end of "Montana Half Light," you had come to appreciate the sky as something more than visual.

In concert, Aaberg explained that last tune was inspired by a fly fishing trip on the Marias River, just a few miles south of his native Chester. Toward evening, he had rounded a bend in the river and glanced up to see the pale silhouette of a deer against the last light of day.

It is a long journey from the Marias River and the Sweetgrass Hills to Oakland, California, where he now lives and works, composing his own music, writing movie soundtracks and recording on the Windham Hill label. But Aaberg is never far from Montana in spirit, and gets back home whenever he can. He traces his success to a supportive hometown and a mother who recognized his talent at an early age. Chester Postmistress Helen Ann Aaberg made sure that if anything got in the way of her son's development, it would not be the fact that Chester is miles from the kind of talent and training a serious musician requires. Every other Sunday, he boarded the train for Spokane, where he took piano lessons on Monday afternoon, caught the Spokane Symphony Monday night and rolled back into Chester late Tuesday morning.

"Not only did I have an understanding school but an understanding town," he said of the leniency he was afforded by Chester school administrators. As with all artists, however, most of Aaberg's success comes from within. "I remember coming home from church one Sunday when I was four and pounding out a Gregorian chant until I got it right," he said. "It felt good, like something I wanted to do for a while."

It was during what she describes as a dry period—one of those dreadful times in the life of an artist when nothing seems to work—that Dana Boussard began thinking about her childhood home and what it meant to her. She was living in San Francisco at the time, having moved there from New York City, where she had been producing small, contemporary paintings and drawings that had "almost a pop art kind of a feeling to them."

In an effort to rekindle the creative fire, she forced herself to do a drawing a day. What began to emerge from her San Francisco studio were images of the area around Choteau—buffalo jumps, cattle drives, prairies, mountains, grainfields, clouds and sky.

She is still producing those images, but today they are coming out of a large studio at her home

124

Above: *Dana Boussard lives in Arlee, on the Flathead Indian Reservation and just a few miles down the road from the National Bison Range at Moiese.* **Top:** *"Cattle Drive Through Choteau II," fabric construction art by Boussard.* **Facing page:** *Horse breeder Tom Eaton of Nye says a good cowboy poem starts out as a line that "nags at you."*

on the Flathead Indian Reservation, six miles south of Arlee in the Jocko Valley. It takes a large studio to accommodate Boussard's work. About once a month, she turns out a finished piece of framed fiber construction that measures anywhere from 3 feet by 5 to 9 feet by 55. Once it leaves her studio, it is shipped to a public building or large, corporate office, frequently outside of Montana.

"Public space art" is what she calls it, and it is different from the kind of art people seek in museums and galleries. Adorning the walls of airport terminals, hospitals and government buildings, Boussard's art is addressed to "people who are coming through a building, not looking specifically for art." Unless they are late for the plane, they usually stop for a closer look at the soft textures and colors that have caught their eyes. "What's going on here?" is the first question that comes to mind when you find yourself in front of one of Boussard's mural-size fabric designs.

Invariably, the design is a statement about Montana. Using familiar symbols, Boussard cuts, paints and stitches pieces of tightly-napped cotton velvet into almost primitive designs. Long, linear heads, magpies, upside-down cows, farmers tangled in ropes are just some of the recurring symbols she uses to convey her response to a drought or a fire or her husband's new interest in Arabian horses. The common denominator in her work is the relationship between people and the land and environment of Montana.

"A lot of what Montana is is what Montana was when it was inhabited only by Indians," she said. "In Montana, it's a lot easier to imagine what it was like at that time than it is in other places that have been overrun by humanity and technology."

It is hard to tell the real cowboys from the would-be cowboys at the annual Montana Cowboy Poetry Gathering but it does not really matter. It is the event that counts—the oral tradition—more than the people who keep it alive.

A century and more after the first Texas trail drive brought cowboys to Montana, the tradition is very much alive here and throughout the West. In 1987, the National Cowboy Poetry Gathering in Elko, Nevada drew 10,000 spectators to an event that was only four years old. Asked to explain its sudden popularity, Hal Cannon, director of the Utah-based Western Folklife Center, said simply: "People respond to a good story.

"In a popular culture like ours, where everything is instantaneous and homogeneous, cowboy poetry is important," he added. "It demonstrates that rural people think, not just urban people and college professors."

It also demonstrates the importance of education and elocution to the West's early families.

"My mother was trained in elocution and she got me started reciting poetry at an early age," said Tom Eaton, a real cowboy who breeds horses on his ranch outside of Nye. "I've used it ever since, around campfires, at dude ranches, in classrooms." Eaton said a good cowboy poem starts out as just a line that "nags at you" for weeks and weeks, as in, *"Riding into the sunset's glow, Just my pony and me..."* At some point, he warned, you have to finish it and commit it to writing.

Hanneke Ippisch, artisan, Huson:

"Most Montanans, especially men, are quiet. They observe everything and take it in but they don't talk about it much. They listen to Montana; they hear it."

MICHAEL CRUMMETT

MICHAEL CRUMMETT PHOTOS BOTH PAGES

Above: *Rodeo has been good and bad to this bull rider.*
Top: *Cowboys at the end of the day.*

"You've got to marry a thought before it gets away, just like you have to marry a pretty woman before she's gone."

For some cowboys, poetry and music are the best means they have of communicating with the rest of the world. "Spending as much time as they do alone and isolated, many cowboys are reticent and shy around other people," said Bob Yarger, a cowboy singer who runs a cattle, sheep and grain operation near Circle. "Poetry readings give them an opportunity to share what's on their mind with other people."

For whatever reason they are drawn to it, Montana's cowboy poets are flourishing. "Montana seems to have more cowboy poets than any other western state," said Montana State Folklorist Michael Korn. "If you kick a sagebrush in Montana, a jackrabbit runs out one side and a cowboy poet out the other."

Like the Democrat who confessed he voted for Reagan in 1984 because he made his living as a political cartoonist and needed the material, Bozeman satirist Greg Keeler is awash in what he regards as the mythology of Montana. Since moving here in 1975, he has studied the Montana "type" as only an outsider can, and dished it out live, on tape and in three volumes of poetry. From buckaroos and "fossil-fuel cowboys" to worm fishermen and fly fishing's elite, no one is immune to Keeler's acid rhymes.

Reincarnation *by Wallace McRae*

Rosebud County rancher Wally McRae is one of Montana's best-known cowboy poets. His "Reincarnation" has been widely published, recited and recorded.

A real cowboy.

W hat does reincarnation mean?"
A cowpoke asked his friend.
His pal replied, "It happens when
Yer life has reached its end.
They comb yer hair and warsh yer neck,
And clean yer fingernails,
And lay you in a padded box
Away from life's travails."

"The box and you goes in a hole,
That's been dug in the ground.
Reincarnation starts in when
Yore planted 'neath a mound
Them clods melt down, just like yer box,
And you who is inside,
And then yore just beginnin' on
Yer transformation ride."

"In a while, the grass'll grow
Upon yer rendered mound.
'Till some day on yer moldered grave
A lonely flower is found.
And say a hoss should wander by,
And graze upon this flower,
That once was you, but now's become
Yer vegetative bower."

"The posey that the hoss done ate
Up, with his other feed,
Makes bone, and fat, and muscle
Essential to the steed.
But some is left that he can't use,
And so it passes through,
And finally lays upon the ground.
This thing, that once was you."

"Then say, by chance, I wanders by,
And sees this on the ground.
And I ponders, and I wonders at,
This object that I found.
And I thinks of reincarnation.
Of life, and death, and such.
I come away concludin': Slim,
You ain't changed, all that much."

Right: *Siesta time on the Padlock Ranch in Big Horn County.*
Below, left: *Glenda Reynolds is a working cowgirl in the Big Open country.*
Right: *Waiting his turn at the Miles City Bucking Horse Sale.*

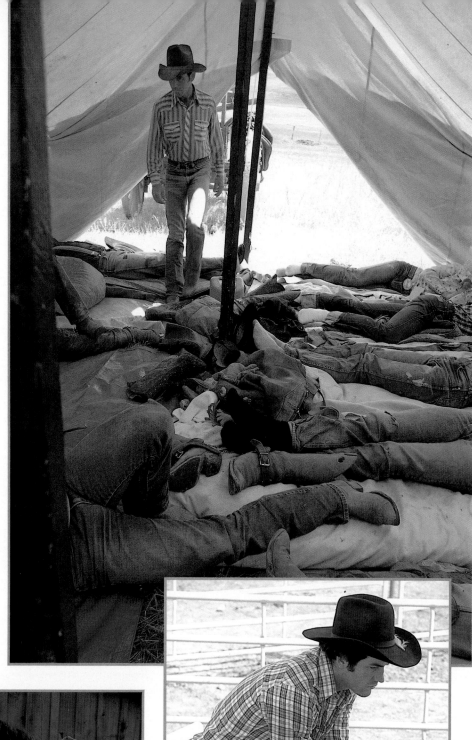

Former bronc-riding champ Lynn Taylor now rides herd on the Pryor Mountain Wild Horse Range.

"I like posing the myth against what I actually see," said Keeler, an associate professor of English at Montana State University. "There are all these illusions about Montanans—the cowboys, the Indians, the fishermen. You see a lot of people like that, but they are just here temporarily to ski. The real cowboys wear ball caps and tennis shoes."

Like the mischievous boy who pulls the pigtails of the girl next door to show his affection, Keeler regards his poems and tunes as an expression of love for his adopted state. A native of Oklahoma, he loves to fish and was "totally amazed" to find a satisfying job in Montana where fishing is at least as important as earning a living. In much of his poetry, Keeler employs fishing as a metaphor to examine the relationships of people, one to another and to their environment. Two of his poems follow on pages 130-131.

Marshall Lambert has been collecting rocks and bones and fossils ever since he began riding the range of Southeastern Montana as a kid. He has been asking questions ever since. Questions like, why are the highest buttes and bluffs in Carter County made up of the same kind of sand found in streambeds? Or, why were there no horses here when Columbus discovered America, when specimens on display in the Carter County Museum indicate horses roamed the area 40 million years ago?

"I'm concerned about the evidence of life," said the retired Ekalaka high

We Montanans

Ode to the Other *by Greg Keeler*

MICHAEL CRUMMETT

Bozeman poet and satirist Greg Keeler pokes fun at cowboys, fishermen and other Montana "types."

When I steal a weekday
from work and drive pavement
to gravel to dirt so the river
might be mine alone,
you're there
from miles of water
splashing upstream toward me,
lunging to beat me
to the foot of the riffle.
If I'm fishing bait, you'll have flies
and eye me coldly under your
L.L. Bean hat. If I'm fishing flies,
you'll sling your sculpin to the foot
of my streamer's swing.
If I'm sick of the world,
you'll ask me how I'm doing
and show me your fat creel.
If they're not biting,
you'll follow my retreat upstream,
telling me that I should
have been here yesterday.
If I've caught a three pounder,
you'll tell me about the four pounder
you just released.
If you come too close,
something will go wrong with my reel,
and I will scream obscenities at it
until you go away.
I've always tried to avoid you,
hiding in alder thickets,
hiking miles to the heart
of wilderness meadows, but
it's no good. You're always there,
clashing with my mood,
darting for my holes,
catching me glancing sideways
while you catch my fish,
sullenly watching me gloat
as I catch yours.
I suppose you're as close
as I'll ever come to death
before death: that long river
leading deep into willow thickets,
hours into darkness,
and you, sloshing up out of brambles,
your waders sucking mud like the sound
of mating pigs to ask, "Having any luck?
What you using? Should have been here yesterday."

The Missouri *by Greg Keeler*

MICHAEL H. FRANCIS

On your first dam at Toston
a farmer took his life
in spite of his lush fields
where you backed up green
then spun down on the heads
of spawning rainbows.
We still see them,
shaking in mist above the
torrent, swimming nowhere
to a home in their heads.
The farther we move
down the divide you drain
the clearer our mistakes
become in your opacity.
Your rims and breaks
dwarf our own erosions.
Coming out of your late youth,
flashing gold-eye in your
sluggish green, you slow down
at Fort Peck to swell
what's behind in losses
the size of giant northerns.
Below that dam, paddlefish
flop out their prehistoric comedy
sucking silt through their gills
for a living. You know that
joke too, rolling your shoulders
one last time, then moving on
to the hard work of the flatlands.

DOUG DYE

Above: *A passionate fisherman, Keeler was "totally amazed" to find work in Montana, where fishing is at least as important as making a living.*
Right: *The Missouri River below Fort Benton.*

school science teacher, who presides over one of the most unusual county museums in the nation. Paleontological specimens that rival some of the nation's best collections are seen by only 2,000 to 3,000 visitors who find their way each year to Ekalaka, at the end of Highway 7 in Montana's extreme southeast corner.

The museum's centerpiece is the 35-foot-long skeleton of a duck-billed dinosaur called Anatosaurus, which roamed the marshlands of Eastern Montana 65 million years ago. Lambert put in 10 years, between 1946 and 1956, assembling the bones, which were collected west of Ekalaka by his predecessor at the museum, Walter Peck. Other specimens include Triceratops, a large-horned dinosaur; Pachycephalosaurus, a Bonehead dinosaur and Mosasaurus, a giant marine lizard.

Lambert shares the nation's fascination with dinosaurs but he is more excited about the newest discovery in the neighborhood, the Mill Iron Site east of Ekalaka, which is turning up the oldest evidence of humanity in Southeastern Montana. According to Lambert, the 11,000-year-old archaeological site shows how ancient peoples killed and butchered bison.

Most people view Ekalaka as the end of the line, a place where the only thing to do is run a few cows or raise some sheep. For an amateur paleontologist like Lambert or the field crews that come out each summer from Princeton and other universities, Ekalaka holds the promise of excitement and scientific discovery. Of his lifelong avocation, Lambert said: "This is a very young science, it's now."

MICHAEL CRUMMETT

Above: *Amateur paleontologist Marshall Lambert keeps early Montana history alive at an unusual museum in Ekalaka.*
Facing page: *The area around Ekalaka, including the Chalk Buttes, is rich with evidence of prehistoric Montana.*

At a time when national journalists travel in packs to compete for the same stories and a national newspaper leaves some readers feeling hungry after they have digested the contents, a good local newspaper, radio or television station is a welcome companion. Here are three that have earned the loyalty of their Montana listeners, readers and viewers.

KSEN Radio, Shelby. Listeners never know who is going to show up on the air at KSEN Radio in Shelby. It could be one of the sales staff, calling in a story from a mobile unit in Cut Bank or Conrad. It could be an oil worker, calling from Sunburst, where he has just witnessed a wreck. It could be one of KSEN's 20 volunteer "weather watchers" who has called to warn westbound travelers that a storm is brewing in the mountains of Glacier Park. Or maybe it is Art Odden, a local meter reader, whose Keilloresque commentary on the human condition has become so popular that it airs twice daily.

"Our listeners don't like to turn the radio off because they're afraid they're going to miss something," said KSEN General Manager Jerry Black, who has assembled a staff of 15 salespeople and broadcasters who cover the Golden Triangle of North-central Montana the way the national press corps covers a New Hampshire primary. No event is insignificant, no angle unexplored. School lunch menus, bus schedules, graduate salutes, birthdays and anniversaries are all part of the daily fare at KSEN.

Co-owner Bob Norris signs on at 5:30 a.m. with a brand of humor that reflects years of experience in front of a microphone. "It's so dry up here, we've

JOHN REDDY

Bob Norris and Jerry Black blend "news, sports, farm and fun" at their Shelby radio station.

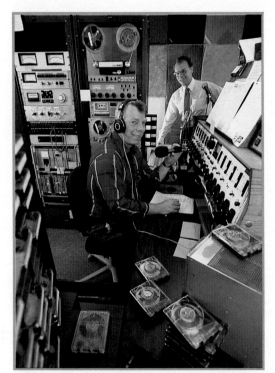

MICHAEL CRUMMETT PHOTOS

The Great Falls Tribune's T.J. Gilles is Montana's only full-time agriculture reporter among general-circulation newspapers.

got trees fighting over the dogs," he said, greeting his farm and ranch audience to a new day. Working up some enthusiasm for this year's KSEN-sponsored U.S. Open Gopher Derby, he gave a quick overview of the event and a rundown of the rules: "We have an outstanding stable of racing gophers this year. The racetrack is as long as a highway is wide, so the entries start training every spring by running back and forth across the highway. On race day, we use a diesel horn to start 'em because that's what they're used to."

Manager Black is at the studio every morning to deliver the 8 o'clock news. Formally titled "Viewing Montana," the Jerry Black morning news show is a hit with the local audience, which has dubbed the show "Chewing Montana" because of Black's chronic pronunciation problems. "Through the years, I've made some great boners," he admitted. "I don't know if people listen for the news or because they want to know how I'm going to mangle the next sentence."

"The thing that welds us together is a good sense of humor," said Norris. "We emphasize four things at KSEN: news, sports, farm and fun."

For all the humor, KSEN has one of the hardest-working, most aggressive news organizations of any radio station in Montana. Its five-day, around-the-clock coverage of the 1964 floods earned a national journalism award. Its live, play-by-play coverage of everything from football and basketball to volleyball, wrestling and track for seven different high schools in a five-county area has earned kudos from both broadcasters and educators. "If it moves, we cover it," said Norris. "We are absolutely the first and main source of news for our listeners," Black added. "We are their neighbor, we're part of the family."

Great Falls Tribune *Farm & Ranch Section.* Whether he is analyzing the contradictions of the latest farm program or exploring the human dimension of Montana's top industry, T.J. Gilles covers the agriculture beat like it's never been covered in a state that should cover it best.

Here is Gilles on the subject of U.S. farm policy: "We pay generous subsidies to Southern tobacco growers—while spending millions more on campaigns begging people not to smoke and covering the emphysema bills with Medicaid."

On the subject of farmers' and ranchers' penchant for documenting the events of their lives: "The wall calendar is a daily encyclopedia of running history. Beneath the Ace Reid cartoon or the scenic photo and logo of the local co-op, one will find each day's square annointed with the eartag numbers of heifers which calved that morning or appeared to be in heat, fields that were planted or cultivated or sprayed that day."

STEPHEN H. ELLIS

ABOVE AND RIGHT: JOHN REDDY

Right: *The Missouri River is an important recreation area for Great Falls residents.*
Above: *A well kept farm in North-central Montana.*
Top: *Great Falls is the major trade center for Montana's Golden Triangle grain-growing region.*

Gilles found an outlet for his opinions back in the late 1960s, as editor of the University of Montana student newspaper, the *Montana Kaimin*. Twenty years later, the Farm & Ranch Section is the perfect forum for his observations of everything from movies and religion to politics. Blaming America's social and economic demise on the nation's preoccupation with golf, he exhorts golfers to "beat those clubs into plowshares. Turn those fairways back into hay meadows. Quit wasting your time on the links and do something constructive."

Gilles puts the Farm & Ranch Section to bed every Thursday. On Sunday, it appears in nearly 45,000 Montana homes as part of the Sunday edition of the *Great Falls Tribune*. Anywhere from four to 12 pages, the tabloid is loaded with news and practical information ranging from market trends and crop and livestock prices to the latest in artificial-insemination techniques and Montana standings in national winter wheat competition. A weekly moisture report, a calendar of events, color photos and profiles of cattle breeders, trout farmers and organic wheat growers extend the appeal of the Farm and Ranch Section to urban and rural readers alike.

Orville Quick, museum curator, Circle:

"God made Eastern Montana; with the leftover pieces, He piled 'em up and made Western Montana."

The ag beat comes naturally to Gilles, who grew up on a small farm-ranch operation outside of Laurel. He is the only full-time agriculture reporter among the state's general-circulation newspapers.

"If I had a lot of money, it would be nice to get back to the ranch," he said. In the meantime, he lives the life vicariously by writing about it. Gilles started writing at a young age. "At one time, I thought I had something to say," he said in the same wry voice that colors much of his writing. He has had offers from larger-circulation newspapers outside the state, but none has been good enough to uproot him.

"I had one pretty good offer," he said, "but when I asked them where the nearest mountain was, there was a long pause at the other end of the line…and here I am." In a 1987 column about the grass-is-greener-elsewhere battle that goes on at one time or another in the minds of most Montanans, Gilles concluded "I've begun to realize that I'm at the point where I have it all—or about all I need, anyway."

KULR-TV , Billings. There is an axiom among broadcast journalists in Montana: Either you have to leave broadcasting or you have to leave Montana. KULR-TV News Director Dave Rye stands out as one who has done neither.

One of the smallest television markets in the nation, Montana is seen as a training ground for broadcast journalists who aspire to news and anchor positions in larger, metropolitan markets. Since he joined KULR in 1980, Rye has seen his news staff of about a dozen—one of Montana's largest—turn over three times.

It is not that he hasn't had offers himself. It is just that he's not looking. Borrowing a Steinbeck quote about how difficult it is "to analyze love when you're in it," Rye tried to explain his attachment to the state. "I don't hunt or fish, so I'm not a typical Montanan," he said. "It's the feeling of community, like a psychological thread that runs through the

Above: *Television news coverage is competitive in Billings, Montana's largest city.*
Facing page: *KULR-TV News Director Dave Rye has defied the broadcasters' axiom: either you leave broadcasting or you leave Montana.*

whole state. There's not a city you can go to where you don't know someone." Apologizing for what is beginning to sound like a chamber of commerce pitch, Rye concluded by saying that all the cliches about friendliness and neighborliness just happen to be true in Montana. "Even politics has a sense of neighborliness here," he said.

Rye's steady presence and his enthusiasm for a beat that covers Montana's southeast quadrant come through on "Straight-8" evening news, making it one of Montana's most popular local news programs. For years, KULR dominated the Billings market, but another Billings station, KTVQ, has come on strong in the ratings with its own local news coverage. Still, Rye believes KULR offers a superior product and traces it to his own longevity: "We know the players better, we know where the bodies are buried; we can relate current events better to the history of the area."

Montanans are rewriting their history with the help of Laurie Mercier, an oral historian who believes that ordinary folk are as important as presidents and kings. "For too long, history has been written by elitists," said Mercier.

"We've been taught that our lives aren't valid unless we're 'important'." Mercier, who worked as the state's first oral historian from 1981 to 1988, has traveled to nearly every town in Montana—she said she can count the towns she has not visited on one hand—and interviewed more than 600 Montanans. Smelter towns, lumber towns, mining towns, railroad towns, farm and ranch communities. All are rich veins of history, waiting to be tapped by someone with a tape recorder and a genuine interest in people.

Working for the Montana Historical Society, Mercier spent nearly as much time training others how to conduct interviews as she did conducting her own. Interpreting interviews and making them available to others is one of the most satisfying aspects of her work. "I think it's important to share these stories with people," she said.

One of her projects—a study of the metals manufacturing industry—explored the relationship between industry and community in Anaconda, East Helena, Black Eagle and Columbia Falls. The result was a traveling exhibit called "The Stack Dominated Our Lives," which combines excerpts from a hundred interviews and 50 historical photographs of life and work during Montana's industrial era.

"History is ambiguous; it's not black and white," said Mercier. "One of the themes that emerged from the metals project is that smelter workers and their families loved the company and they hated the company."

In other projects, Mercier has explored life in a dozen of Montana's small towns, Montanans at work during the early 1900s, the role of women's organizations in Montana history, Billings' Hispanic community and the work of Indian educators. More recently, she has been studying the impact of the New Deal on Montana by interviewing people who were involved with government projects during the 1930s.

Mercier began studying oral history as a graduate student after teaching at a black school in Memphis, Tennessee. "My students couldn't read or write, so I got them to interview their grandparents and bring their stories back to the classroom," she said. "I see oral history as an empowerment. People have a lot of sense; it's just a matter of providing them with the skills to write their own history."

Above: *Oral historian Laurie Mercier believes ordinary folk are as important as presidents and kings.*
Facing page, top: *Retired smelterworkers, like these Anaconda residents, are a rich source of history for anyone with a tape recorder and a genuine interest in people.*
Bottom: *Bigfork potter David Shaner lives in Montana because "This is what I want to be influenced by, and what I want to make my symbols from."*

There are artists and there are merchants of art. The merchants may be good craftsmen, but they are likely to get stuck on a design or a pattern that sells. The artists keep growing, their evolving work seen and collected as art.

When David Shaner decided to build a home and studio and kiln in Montana, just north of Bigfork, he realized he was making a commitment to build and throw pots for a living. He also realized that "there was more to life than glazing pots with Shaner's Red and selling them in mountain gift shops." Looking back on his evolution from a ceramics student in Pennsylvania to a full-time potter in Montana, he said he has also become aware of the "contrast between simply the production of more wares and the organic growth of self."

MICHAEL CRUMMETT PHOTOS BOTH PAGES

One of the ironies of Shaner's work, which appeals to sophisticated audiences on both the east and west coasts, is its simplicity. "At one time when I'd send pots to a show they would always invite a few way-out potters to round things out," he wrote in a 1979 issue of *Studio Potter*. "Now it seems that most of the shows are way-out, and they invite me or someone else to throw in a conservative piece."

Shaner describes his work as functional or "vessel-oriented." If it is not functional, it "hints at being functional," he said. His forms are rounded and simple, his colors are the colors of the earth.

Writing in a 1983 issue of *American Craft*, ceramicist Daniel Rhodes said of Shaner's pottery: "That his work is almost universally admired should not arouse the suspicion that it is somehow shallow or ordinary. It is admirable in the same way that a mountain, a lake, or a cloud is admirable; we are captivated by its shape and color, and we know exactly what it is for."

Beyond mountains, lakes and clouds, the minerals, birds and plants of his Bigfork home nourish Shaner's spirit and inspire his work. Every aspect of his hand-wrought home, from its terraced

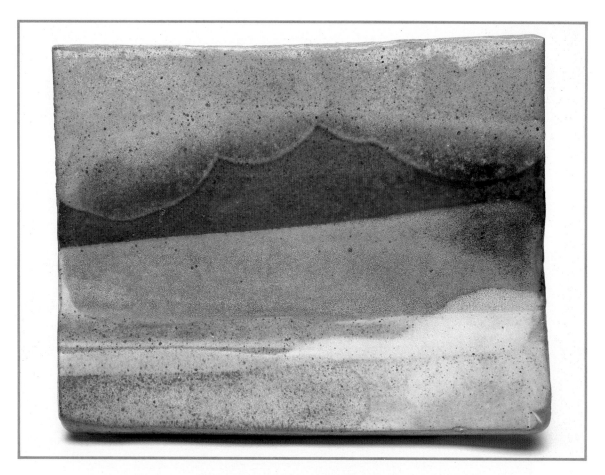

rock gardens to the sunny, plant-lined deck that overlooks a pine forest at the north edge of the Swan Range, betrays the artist's effort to surround himself with the natural world.

"At one time, I noticed potters were painting bamboo and palm trees on their pots," he said. "I thought that was kind of silly. Your work is a reflection of your environment. I live here because this is what I want to be influenced by, and what I want to make my symbols from."

Thirty years after he first discovered the satisfaction of creating beauty from clay, Shaner admits he used to worry about running out of ideas. "Now, I worry that there isn't enough time to do all that I want to do."

Bill Stockton has been known to tell his poolroom friends that he really doesn't know whether he is "an artist who ranches or a rancher who arts." Under interrogation, he will tell you that his art was never meant to be a vocation. "It's something to do," he said. "It has no more importance than knitting."

MICHAEL CRUMMETT

Above: *Grassrange sheepman Bill Stockton doesn't know whether he is "an artist who ranches or a rancher who arts."*
Facing page: *David Shaner's forms are rounded and simple, his colors the colors of the earth.*

Regardless of their importance, Stockton's drawings, paintings, sculpture and writing have provided him with an endless source of diversion and fun out on the range of Central Montana. Of the drawings that appear in a whimsical book called *Ewe-Phemisms*, the Grassrange sheepman told his readers: "I had a ball doing them and maybe you can, also, participate in my snickers, moans & groans." Earlier, readers had a ball with *Today I Baled Some Hay to Feed the Sheep the Coyotes Eat*, a sheepman's humorous and indelicate insights into an animal he clearly adores.

"Any dumb bastard can run a cow, but it takes an intellectual to raise a sheep," he said, describing a sheep as a "pacific animal that is utterly dependent on you." He regards ranching as "the most complex business you can get into," and explains: "There are a thousand-thousand-thousand-thousand bits of information you have to carry in your head. Within five minutes, you have to decide if there is going to be a birth and how much weather a new lamb can take. You have to have had one die, and then you have to remember it. You have to make judgments that a computer can't make."

Stockton did not start raising sheep until he was 40 years old. After growing up on ranches in nearby Winnett and Grassrange, he became an army medic during World War II, stationed in Paris. There, he met his wife, Elvia, whom he transplanted to Grassrange after the war. "We had just come through a very cold winter in France," Elvia recalled nearly 40 years later, "and Bill promised me it would be warm in Montana." A gracious woman who looks and sounds more French than American, Elvia is thoroughly at home in Grassrange.

Before returning to Montana, Stockton studied art in Paris and Minneapolis. He has experimented with nearly every medium, ranging from watercolors and oil pastels to neon design and metal sculpture. One of his favorite instruments is a cattle marker, a giant chalky crayon used to mark livestock, which he combines with oil pastels to achieve bold colors and designs. He is currently teaching himself how to make felt from sheep's wool and transform it into clothing.

Stockton's art has been exhibited throughout Montana, in the Midwest

Bill Stockton believes "any dumb bastard can run a cow, but it takes an intellectual to raise a sheep."

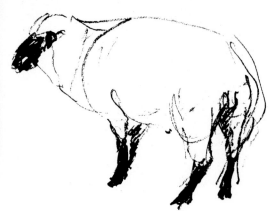

DRAWINGS BY BILL STOCKTON

and on the West Coast. His sculptures, paintings and drawings appear in public buildings and private homes from Montana to Paris. But he does not have much use for the art world, which he regards as "phony." He leads a sophisticated, if schizophrenic life, traveling occasionally from Grassrange to Paris to visit his in-laws. But he is at peace when he is in Grassrange, where he and Elvia still delight in the miracle of a newborn lamb or a brood of chicks. After a recent trip to Paris, he shook his head about the living conditions and described apartments as "concrete blocks stacked on top of one another where people need three keys to get in the door."

"Those people are prisoners," he said. "It makes you realize how free we are. It is a great privilege to live out here."

As a child, Agnes Vanderburg accompanied her family every fall into what is now known as the Bob Marshall Wilderness to gather meat, fish and berries. After the meat was dried, they returned to the Flathead Indian Reservation, where hides were turned into buckskins, leggings and moccasins. The last time she made that trip with her family was 1923. "My sister and son tell me it's changed a lot," said the Flathead Reservation Indian elder. "They say the campgrounds have names and the trails are rutted and dusty."

If the wilderness has changed since 1923, the world beyond its boundaries is beyond recognition. But there is a remote camp on the Flathead Reservation where you can still see what the world was like when Agnes was a child. Every summer, people from around the globe travel to "Agnes Camp" to learn the old ways from one of the few Flathead elders who is still able to pass them along.

For nearly 20 years, Agnes has been holding court at her camp, just a few miles northwest of Arlee near the National Bison Range. There, she teaches anyone who is interested in learning how to build a tepee, smoke and tan a hide and collect and cure natural herbs from the hills nearby. In 1987, she had 3,000 students. Some stayed a week; some stayed all summer. Some came from as near as the reservation; some came from as far away as Germany and Iran.

At 87, Agnes still smokes cigarettes but avoids the other evils of the marketplace. "I get scared of eating away from home," she said. She still relies on wild game provided by her boys and the berries and herbs she collects during the summer. Her face wrinkles into a grin when she describes how she has rid someone of warts or ulcers with the right herbal treatment. "I teach what I know," she said as simply as the life she lives.

When James Welch writes about a hapless Indian who goes to Buttrey's to buy a can of tomato soup only to learn from the clerk that today is Thanksgiving, he describes the world next door and a million miles away. For nearly 20 years, poet and novelist Welch has been sharing with a growing readership his insights and experiences about life on the reservation.

A native of Browning, Welch is the son of Blackfeet and Gros Ventre Indians. Having grown up on both the Blackfeet and Fort Belknap reservations, he regards them as "extremely beautiful at the right time of the year," but he prefers to write about them from a distance.

MICHAEL CRUMMETT

People come from around the globe to learn the "old ways" from Flathead elder Agnes Vanderburg.

In his second novel, *The Death of Jim Loney*, Welch writes about reading and learning as a kind of salvation for "two half-breed kids caught in the slack water of a minor river." That's what his education meant to him. After a "bottomed-out" cattle market forced his family off their Fort Belknap farm in the 1950s, they moved to Minneapolis, where his dad worked as a welder. Welch graduated from high school there and attended one year of college before moving back to Montana, where he spent two years at Northern Montana College and graduated from the University of Montana. He has lived in Missoula ever since with his wife of 20 years, Lois, who teaches English at UM and directs the university's creative writing program.

Poet-novelist James Welch regards his love-hate relationship with Montana as an ally: "It brings a lot of conflict into my writing and that's good."

Welch's interest in poetry developed in high school, where he wrote a lot of "mushy things in rhymed couplets." It was not until he came under the influence of the late Richard Hugo at UM that he became a serious poet. "He was my real inspiration," he said of Hugo. "He taught me that an ordinary guy like myself had something to say about my life and my people."

Much of the credit for his skill as a novelist, he said, goes to UM's William Kittredge. Welch's first novel, *Winter in the Blood*, was born out of an all-night critique during which "Bill told me all the things that were not good about it, page by page." Discouraged at the time, Welch put the manuscript away "forever." A month later he pulled it out, wrote two more drafts and sold it to Harper & Row. "Looking back, I realize that Bill virtually gave me a short course in one night on how to write a novel," he said.

Welch is working on his fourth novel, this one about an Indian lawyer based in Helena. "I'm trying to write about a successful Indian this time," he said. The price of success is the guilt his protagonist feels about leaving the reservation and the "people back home," and like his earlier work, is "mildly autobiographical." Welch still has family on Fort Belknap and visits often but said, "I couldn't live there for a week." While he has made a break from the reservation, he would be hard put to leave Montana: "I can't think of another state that would stimulate me as a writer the way this state does." He talks of a love-hate relationship with Montana, one he thinks is shared by many Montanans, and regards it as an ally: "It brings a lot of conflict into my writing and that's good."

Gary Zowada has the notion that if history is going to repeat itself, then we might as well have some fun with it. He's been doing just that since 1981 when, in his mid-20s, he became director of the Big Horn County Historical Museum and Visitor Center in Hardin.

"I once heard a child who, when asked if he wanted to visit a museum, said, 'No, I don't want to go to a dead zoo'," said the youthful Zowada, trying to explain his approach to historic preservation. "We're not a dead zoo; we're an activity center."

Hi-Line images like these have inspired Welch's writing for nearly 20 years.

Since Zowada came on the scene, the museum is also one of Hardin's major industries. The day it opened in 1978 on five acres of donated land, the museum drew 300 visitors. By 1987, 23,000 tourists a year were taking the Hardin exit from I-90 to view the not-so-old West at the museum's wild game feeds, street dances, fiddlers' jamborees or perhaps the Undercover Girls' annual quilt show. Spread over 24 acres, the museum includes a Crow log cabin, a 1922 schoolhouse, a 1917 general store, a 1917 German Lutheran church, a 1900 railroad depot, another half-dozen authentic buildings and a large park. The buildings are put to use regularly for weddings, recitals and kids' field trips.

"If someone had told me in high school that I'd be a museum director in Hardin by the time I was 30, I wouldn't have believed it," said Zowada. In fact, it was the year he graduated from Hardin High that the die was cast. Having lived there only three years, he wondered why the town, with its rich heritage and cultural diversity, didn't have a museum. He voiced his query in a letter to the editor and, bingo, he was the guy Hardin had been looking for. Before he could even think about college, he had his first full-time job as director of the fledgling museum and visitor center.

Big Horn County Museum and Visitor Center Director Gary Zowada became Hardin's first museum director shortly after he graduated from high school. In a letter to the editor, he had wondered out loud why Hardin, with its rich history and cultural diversity, did not have a museum.

The biggest problem he faces today is how to obtain a college degree while running one of Southeastern Montana's busiest tourist attractions. He has been squeezing in classes when he can at Rocky Mountain College in Billings. Weary of what he describes as the "extended college plan," he has decided to leave the museum and Montana so he can complete two more years of schooling for a degree in history and business administration. He hopes to return because "Montana is my first love and always will be."

Crow Country is coal country and cattle country.

In many respects, Montana has been an opera waiting to happen. From prospectors and prostitutes to cattle barons and copper kings, there has been no shortage of drama. Larger-than-life characters, unresolved conflicts and a compelling story are all necessary elements of good opera. Add a musical score, an orchestra, a chorus and a booming baritone or mezzo-soprano, and Montana's colorful history would be ready for the live stage.

If it were that easy, Montana's arts community wouldn't be as excited as it is about "Pamelia," a Montana-made opera about the woman behind one of the men who pioneered the West. "Pamelia" was conceived in 1983, when Bozeman writers Linda Peavy and Ursula Smith began researching correspondence between separated husbands and wives that dated back to the gold-rush era. Having published two collective biographies and made numerous presentations on "the extraordinary accomplishments of ordinary women," Peavy and Smith had begun making a name for themselves as biographers of history's unsung women.

MICHAEL CRUMMETT PHOTOS BOTH PAGES

Bozeman's Linda Peavy, Ursula Smith and Eric Funk have written and composed an opera set in Montana's gold rush era.

Their research had taken them from library archives to old homestead cabins, where they found clues to the story of Pamelia Fergus, a Minnesota woman who was left behind with four children and a failing business when her husband, James, went West in search of new opportunities. The opera opens with the "Courage" and "Farewell" arias as he departs for Pike's Peak, fully intending to find the gold that will enable him to provide a better living for his family. It ends shortly after he and Pamelia are reunited in Virginia City, Montana Territory, four years later, when he announces he must leave his family again, this time for the gold strike at Prickly Pear. One of thousands of 19th-century women who were temporarily or permanently abandoned by westering husbands, Pamelia was seen by Peavy and Smith as a prototype of the "women in waiting" of the westward movement.

"Her story towered above the rest, for her transformation during James' long absence seemed to be the most dramatic and long-lasting of all the transformations undergone by the women whose lives we had examined," the two wrote in a 1987 issue of *Montana Artpaper*. "We thought about a novel, but the story seemed too fantastic, too much bigger than life to fit between the covers of a novel."

They came upon the idea of an opera while listening to a performance in Bozeman of an orchestral work by Eric Funk, a contemporary composer then living in Portland. Everything about his music was right for the story they were developing so they did the only logical thing: they telephoned him and suggested that he compose the music for their fledgling opera. "We bombarded him over the phone with our thoughts about Pamelia," Smith recalled. "We didn't give him a chance to talk because we were afraid he would say no."

In fact, he said yes. Born in Deer Lodge and raised partly in Lewistown, Funk had been looking for an opportunity to move back to Montana. "Like a salmon swimming upstream, I've spent most of my life trying to get back here," he said of his serendipitous alliance with Peavy and Smith.

Four years later, the musical score and the libretto are finished. The music

Bonnie Lambert, businesswoman, Helena:

"There's a sense of personal history here that you don't find in other places. Montanans are aware of their history and work hard to hang on to it. Even the white crosses on the highways. Some people think they're morbid, but they're just one more way of remembering."

Along U.S. 2, between Libby and Kalispell.

will make its debut at Carnegie Hall in May 1989, when Montana's favorite baritone, Pablo Elvira, will perform several arias from the opera as part of a choral interpretation by a Portland-area chorus under the direction of Jonathan Griffith. Elvira, who sings regularly with the Metropolitan Opera and the New York City Opera, lives in Bozeman during the off-season and is a founder of Montana's Intermountain Opera. Montanans will have an opportunity to enjoy a more extensive preview of the opera in June 1989, when some selections will be performed by the Billings Symphony at the Alberta Bair Theater as part of a six-state Centennial symposium.

To sit around a kitchen table with Peavy, Smith and Funk as they catch one another up on the latest developments of their project is to glimpse at the agony and ecstasy of art in the making. All have made personal sacrifices to get the opera off the ground, and none knows where the money will come from to keep it, or them, going.

"We're a little crazy, like James Fergus leaving his home and family to search for gold," said Peavy. "It was so right, we decided to take the risk of writing and composing it free-lance."

Risks aside, the three view "Pamelia" as the artistic highlight of their careers. "As a composer, I think a piece of music has to be a quantum leap before I consider it worthwhile," said Funk, explaining the challenge of conveying Pamelia's gradual self-discovery and triumph through music.

As writers, Peavy and Smith hope the opera will be toured across the Northwest, paying musical tribute to the roles women played in the settling of the West.

"We're nothing if we're not optimists," said Peavy.

T.J. GILLES

Tirrell at work on We Montanans *at the Chouteau County Fair, Fort Benton, in September 1987.*

Norma Tirrell has spent 17 years writing for newspapers, magazines, private organizations and public interest groups. Currently, she writes and produces tourism publications for the State of Montana. She is a 1971 graduate of the University of Montana School of Journalism. She and her husband, Gordon Bennett, live in Helena. *We Montanans* is her first book.

Michael Crummett is a free-lance photographer who specializes in images of people. After graduating from the University of Kansas in 1970, he studied at the Brooks Institute of Photography for two years. His work has appeared in numerous magazines and books, including *Montana's Indians, Yesterday and Today*, published in 1985 as Number 11 in the Montana Geographic Series. He and his wife, Linda, and their two sons live in Billings.

A.B. Guthrie, Jr., won the Pulitzer Prize for fiction in 1950 with his novel *The Way West*, the second in a series of six novels about the West. Guthrie is a 1923 graduate of the University of Montana with a B.A. in journalism. He and his wife, Carol, live near Choteau.